FRIENDSHIPPING

The Art of

FINDING FRIENDS, BEING FRIENDS, *and* KEEPING FRIENDS

FRIENDSHIPPING

The Art of
FINDING FRIENDS, BEING FRIENDS, *and* KEEPING FRIENDS

JENN BANE *and* **TRIN GARRITANO**

WORKMAN PUBLISHING
NEW YORK

Library of Congress Cataloging-in-Publication Data is available.

ISBN 978-1-5235-0861-7

Design by Becky Terhune

Workman books are available at special discounts when purchased in bulk for premiums and sales promotions as well as for fund-raising or educational use. Special editions or book excerpts can also be created to specification. For details, contact the Special Sales Director at the address below or send an email to specialmarkets@workman.com.

Workman Publishing Co., Inc.
225 Varick Street
New York, NY 10014-4381
workman.com

WORKMAN is a registered trademark of Workman Publishing Co., Inc.

Printed in China
First printing December 2020

10 9 8 7 6 5 4 3 2 1

CONTENTS

Part Three

*"I don't believe that blood makes a family;
kin is the circle you create, hands held tight."*

—TAYARI JONES,
An American Marriage

Introduction

This mic on?

Hello, hello, are we recording?

Looks like we're recording.

I can't hear myself in these headphones.

Hmm, your mic isn't picking up.

Years ago, this book began as a podcast. Whenever we hung out together, we found ourselves discussing friendship, mental health, and our shared goal of becoming kinder people. Discussing these things in front of a microphone seemed kinda fun. If nothing else, it was an excuse to hang out a few more hours a week. We named our show *Friendshipping* and made lots of production errors. To our surprise, emails from listeners began pouring in, all of them asking for our advice. *How do I meet new people and then successfully make plans to hang out with them? Is it terrible that I really want to unfollow my friend on Twitter? Can I break up with a friend I've known since childhood?*

We received thoughtful questions that deserved thoughtful responses. Before hitting "record" each week, we sat down together, opened an empty Google document, and unloaded our thoughts. Over two hundred episodes later, we have pages and pages of notes that we thought might be worth sharing. Podcasts aren't for everyone, after all. What if our notes could help people?

Those notes are now this book. The questions you've asked us are here, too—with edits for space and privacy—so you can see just how universal your concerns about friendship really are.

We hope our advice meets you where you are. While this book has an ending, your interpretations of friendship will not end, nor should they. Your relationships will evolve, your boundaries and priorities will shift, and you will gain and shed friends throughout your life. What was right for you in the past may not be right for you now. The same goes for us: No doubt we'll reread this in five years and cringe because we said this, or forgot that, or failed to consider a perspective. All we want to do is offer ideas, and *you* can decide where they belong. We don't have all the answers—just possibilities. We are not friendship "experts." Those don't even exist. If we hold any authority here at all, it's only because we a) overthink everything, and b) have made many, many mistakes in our own friendships.

Our hope is that this book offers many paths forward, and that one of them feels right for you. Or maybe this book will help you see that you knew the answer all along.

OK, my mic's working now. And we're recording.

PART ONE

On Making Friends
The Basics

Friendship is an ancient survival skill. Millenia ago, Paleolithic humans worked together to find resources, protect one another, and gather food. Scientists think it's possible they formed groups to better hunt woolly mammoths because the animals were ten feet tall and required several arrows and spears to take down. Today, you don't need friends to help you hunt a bison (though maybe some of them would help, if asked), but they do make surviving a whole lot easier.

Biology agrees: Companionship boosts important feel-good chemicals in your brain. You'd think something so essential would be easier to attain in this modern age, especially because there are now about eight billion people on Earth. But while the numbers may be in our favor when it comes to meeting new people, it sure as hell doesn't feel that way. Making friends and keeping them as an adult is really, really hard.

WHY MAKING FRIENDS CAN FEEL SO DIFFICULT

To start, there's no script for you to follow. TV and movies offer us cliché romantic milestones (exchanging phone numbers, asking someone out, the first date, the first smooch), but there's not really an equivalent for friendship. How many times must you hang out together before you can decide you are pals? What's the precise number of text messages that need to be sent before you reach capital-F Friendship? Is there a "third base" for best buds?

Logistics also play a part here. Maybe you live in an isolated area, and transit is an issue. Even if you live in a well-populated place with public transportation, there's probably not a communal place where friends can drop in every day. No dorm room, no Central Perk, no *Cheers* bar. It's tough to even *find* your people—the people whose values, schedules, and lifestyles gel with yours—let alone see them with any regularity. It was different when you were a kid. If you had a conventional childhood, you were surrounded by peers basically all the time. Most of your waking hours were probably spent at school, where you had recess, you were paired up in gym class, and you were forced into group projects. Socializing was built into your education; it was a structured part of your development. As a grown-up, you have to go out of your way to create the circumstances that give you access to new people.

And let's be real: There is a monetary cost to having a social life, and most people don't have those extra funds to spare. Adults often center their lives around making enough money to survive. You can't just pick up a hobby to meet new people, as all traditional advice says, because most hobbies cost money. And while you don't *need* extra money to make new friends, it would certainly make the task easier. If we could wave a magic wand and give you an extra $200 to burn at an arcade or your neighborhood bar, we would in a heartbeat.

But you're too damn busy for that anyway. Imagine that every single responsibility you hold—your job, your health, someone else's health, your inbox, your pets, your overdue homework, paying rent on time—is represented by a bowling ball. Some are light. Some are heavy. But that's gotta be dozens and dozens of bowling balls, right? (A public school teacher once told us that every one of her students = another bowling ball. EESH.) If you suddenly add "make new friends" to your list of obligations, that's like carrying the bowling balls up a set of stairs or a hill. If you are part of a marginalized group of people, you have an even heavier load, more stairs, and steeper hills. Parents are also especially challenged to carve out time for themselves, yet they're taught to feel guilty when they do it. Carrying too much at once can make you collapse, even if you have huge muscles, like us. Also, the polar ice caps are melting at disastrous rates, and why can't any gun control laws pass in the United States? (We hope that sentence will be outdated by the time this book is in print, but probably not.)

With all this in mind, you can see that it isn't fair to blame yourself for not being able to make new friends. (Unless you're a jerk with no redeeming qualities. But you probably aren't. Everyone acts like a jerk sometimes, but that doesn't mean you are one.) There are legitimate obstacles in your way, and you're working with limited time and resources. We're rarely afforded the circumstances that make it easy to establish new friendships. But here's the good news: Making friends does not require you to employ sweeping life changes. It requires effort, sure, but you don't have to throw yourself into a uplifting movie montage where you call up long-lost friends from childhood, jump in the car for a road trip, fill your calendar with extracurriculars, scrub your apartment top to bottom, take out a dozen bags of trash, and get that perfect shiny new haircut. In fact, we don't recommend making many dramatic changes all at once, because that level of commitment is just not sustainable. It's simply time to tweak your habits and behaviors to make your life easier for friend-making.

BEFORE YOU BEGIN

First things first: Before you get to know new people, why not get to know yourself? Understanding yourself is a powerful tool. We encourage you to assess your goals, intentions, good moods, bad moods, and habits, so you can learn how to best set yourself up for success in making friends. Here's a starting point: Have you ever played one of those painful icebreaker games, like Two Truths and a Lie or Never Have I Ever? If you've suffered through a college orientation, this is probably bringing up some awkward memories. But luckily you don't have to do this exercise with anyone else. Start by reflecting on what you would change about your social life and friendships. You can also write it down (and then probably hide it somewhere, or eat the evidence). Be very specific. It's important that you imagine changes that are, in fact, attainable. These are not attainable:

- I want people to like me more, without putting any time into this process or adjusting my approach or expectations.

- I want everybody to know how hilarious I am.
- I want celebrities to follow me on social media, and for my every hot take to go viral.
- I want to be friends with rich and talented people who take me out on their private jet.
- I would like to stop making mistakes forever.
- Like a video game, I would like to go back to the character creation screen and re-roll to get a new face and body.
- I'd like to have twelve close friends who deeply admire me. I want to be Jesus.

But here are some changes that are achievable. Maybe you'd like to:

- Feel more comfortable making small talk
- Feel less embarrassment when you make a mistake
- Put yourself into social situations where you can meet new people
- Stick up for yourself
- Learn how to express your thoughts and emotions more clearly
- Improve your self-confidence
- Get to know your coworkers
- Plan parties and get out more
- Get better at gauging how interested someone is in what you have to say
- Tune your sense of humor to make people laugh

You're focusing on the changes you can actually control, one at a time. When you restore an antique house—not that we ever have, but stay with us—you don't overhaul everything at once. You repaint one windowsill. Then you replace the broken banister, or fix the lightbulbs. Then you make a decision about the flooring, and perhaps you discover something surprising, like there's incredible antique hardwood underneath the linoleum and you want to keep it; you don't want to change what's already there. You upgrade what you want little by little, piece by piece.

To help you along, we'd like you to adopt the habit of "metathinking." (Or "metacognition," if you're an actual psychologist, which we are not.) Metathinking means *thinking about the way you think*. It's a mental tool often used to make students notice their strengths and weaknesses and determine the best way they learn. Here, metathinking means noticing what thoughts enter your mind and examining why they're there, where they came from, and if they are actually true. Your thoughts dictate your mood and self-worth,

so it's important to be mindful of that voice in your head, especially when it's cruel to you. This is particularly useful for anxious people who do a lot of negative self-talk. It is really, really hard to find new pals and try new things when you feel like garbage on the inside. You are not garbage, so do the work you need to do to feel less like garbage.

Here's an example of metathinking in action: Say you're at a hip coffee shop crowded with hotties in cool glasses, and you accidentally spill your iced latte all over a stranger. You apologize, but you spend the rest of the day reliving the moment, feeling embarrassed, and mentally berating yourself. You might think: *I am always so awkward and clumsy and gross. Ughhh!* But the voice inside your head is often an unreliable narrator. Hit your internal pause button. Ask yourself: *Hang on. Is that really true? Do I deserve the way I'm treating myself over a mistake?* Zoom out and look at the thought again. You may start realizing:

- *Well, no one is awkward all the time.*
  That's an exaggeration.
- *And was I really all that awkward?*
- *Why do I accuse myself of being awkward so often?*
- *Being awkward is not that bad, anyway.*
  It's not an awful trait.
- *Aren't human beings allowed to make mistakes?*
  It was just a spill.
- *If I saw someone spill their coffee, wouldn't I have*
  empathy for them? Why can't I have empathy for
  myself in this moment?
- *Oh. I'm dwelling on this tiny situation because my brain*
  is treating it as evidence that I screw everything up.
  But on its own, spilling my coffee isn't a big deal.

The goal of metathinking is to practice compassion for other people *and* for yourself. You do not have to believe all your negative thoughts. And look, we know this feels cheesy, but these mental games are worth the effort. We wish we could all go back in time and get the emotional training we deserved as children. Very few of us received profound childhood education on empathy, consent, self-esteem, and the personhood of others. So we're talking to you, but also to that seven-year-old version of you who deserved better. Do the exercises for younger you. Because when you believe that you are someone who is good enough for human companionship, you will have an easier time making friends. And you deserve friends! You deserve to be cared for and understood. This doesn't mean you get to point to a specific person and say, "I deserve your time and attention. Be my friend now." But you can certainly *develop* companionship that is fulfilling and reciprocated and widespread. Humans need other humans.

WHERE TO START: DEFINING FRIENDSHIP

There's no universally accepted definition of what makes a friend. Even if you feel like there is, we wouldn't want you to devote yourself to one narrow interpretation of what friendship can look like. Otherwise, you will pursue only one type of friendship, or you'll compare your friendships to relationships that aren't feasible or don't make sense for you.

Here's what we do know: In the most basic terms, a friend is someone you actively and joyfully welcome into your life. You've given them some kind of access to you, and they've reciprocated. Maybe you've exchanged social media handles, email addresses, or phone numbers. Friends ask, "How are you?" because they are genuinely curious about the answer. In conversations, they take turns asking questions and show interest in each other's hobbies (or show interest in the fact that you're interested). Friends do not need to participate in all the same things, but they participate in *some* of the same things. They remember facts about each other, like your beloved sports team, or that you dislike horror movies, or at the very least, that you are mortally allergic to pine nuts.

A friend is someone who respects you—your identity, your decisions, your sexuality, how you see the world, and how you choose to spend your time. They accept your personal boundaries and want you to feel comfortable and valued. A friend helps carry your baggage instead of adding to it.

Friends want you to have fun at an event even if they aren't there with you; they want you to have other friends who love you; they do not hold claims to your time or attention. No is an acceptable answer between true friends. Friends are not manipulative, controlling, or abusive, and fights occur rarely.

Friends usually like each other about the same amount, but of course, it is impossible to have perfectly balanced relationships across the board. Sometimes you will feel extremely close to a dear friend, but that dear friend happens to have a best friend who predates you by a few decades. It's not an affront to you that your friend has other people they are close (or closer) to, or have simply known longer.

Dear Friendshipping,

How should I decide who to be friends with? I have only so much time and energy, so if I'm going to make an effort, rather than simply being friendly to whomever happens to be nearby, how should I decide whom to invest in?

Actually, "being friendly to whomever happens to be nearby" is a good place to start if you want to make new friends. (Friend, friendly—look, they even share most of the same letters.) You don't have to be particularly talkative or chummy in order to be friendly, though; perhaps you have a dry sense of humor, or you're very shy, or you don't feel confident with small talk. All good! "Friendly" can simply mean "being openly kind and curious," and that's a productive step toward making new friends. And you're right, you have only so much time and energy; energy comes at a cost and time is a nonrenewable resource. You don't have to continually initiate plans with people you just aren't clicking with. Invest in the people who are kind to you and to others; people with whom you share a hobby or sense of humor; people whose company you enjoy.

Roasting and Pranking:
A NUANCED LOVE LANGUAGE

Friends can make fun of each other without being cruel. Just remember:

- Avoid any potentially harmful or sensitive topics based on the individual. If you don't already have an understanding of what's funny to them and what hurts, you are not yet ready to roast this friend.

- Know the difference between exchanging wits and being hurtful. Make sure your friend is laughing sincerely and jabbin' back at you.

- Make it affectionate. Roasts are usually compliments in comedic disguises.

- You can tease your friends about their meaningless, harmless quirks, like this one: Jenn cannot remember the names or faces of extremely famous actors. She can never remember what movies Clint Eastwood has done. Willem Dafoe? Never heard of him. Friends quiz her on this to see what wild answers she will conjure because they know she doesn't mind.

- If you're roasting a friend because they have a weird habit, frame it as special and interesting. We've got a pal who prefers cereal instead of croutons in his salad. Cereal! It's all about the texture, apparently.

- Roasting invites consequences. One time Trin's brother made fun of her big teeth. In turn, she chewed up a sleeve of Oreos and spit them all over his bed. You reap what you roast.

Just like there isn't a single definition for what makes a friend, there are many examples of what a *best* friend can look like. If you committed a grisly crime (and please do not—our lawyers would like us to say that we are not encouraging this), your closest friends would perhaps top the list of potential accomplices and confidants. A best friend can be your spouse, a sibling, or your group of college friends whom you love equally. Or you might not have a best friend at all. Movies and TV have taught us that everyone has a single best BEST friend, a better half, a top cheerleader, and if you don't, something is probably wrong with you. But you don't have to categorize your friends into gold, silver, and bronze, like the Friend Olympics. You don't require a single "best" friend. You don't need the Abbi to your Ilana, the JD to your Turk, the Molly to your Issa. It's unfair to compare yourself to fictional characters.

A friendship can be low-maintenance, long-distance, temporary, or entirely online. Whether you communicate once a month at bar trivia or every morning over coffee in the break room, that's a friendship. Friendships do not have to be acted upon every single day. Friends don't need to follow each other on social media. You can even have friends you never make formal plans with, but run into at your neighborhood park, for example. Or maybe there are people you see just once a year in Tulsa at the Yarn-A-Thon Knitting Convention. Are these folks going to remember the names of your parents or deliver a heartfelt toast at your next birthday party? Probably not. Are they going to make your list of emergency contacts? Nah. But so what? A friendship can be specific to a setting or context and still be a meaningful connection.

CONSIDER THE FRIENDS
YOU MAY ALREADY HAVE

As you begin your search for new friends, take stock of your flock. What mighty ducks are currently in your flying V? Is there anyone in your life you'd consider an almost-friend? Whom do you want to get to know better? (The answer to these questions might be "literally no one," and that's OK, too; you can start from anywhere.) We've listed some common and recognizable dynamics below that might help you understand yourself and your relationships, both new and old. Do any of these look familiar?

THE FAIRY SQUAD MOTHER/BROTHER/OTHER

This person is the group planner—great at organizing activities, hosting, and nurturing. They can act like a parent or guardian: always taking on the burdens of others. That's so kind to do. Unfortunately, people like this often try to take on *all* the burdens. This kind of friend is prone to burning out, overstepping boundaries, and/or not taking time for themselves.

THE PARTY PAL

This is the type of friend that you meet for drinks or go out to clubs or concerts with. Perfectly nice, enjoyable company, but they're probably not the person you call when you need serious advice or an important favor. Nothing wrong with that. It's great to enjoy a mutually surface-level relationship with someone who knows how to have fun.

THE FANDOM FRIEND

This friend is fanatical about the same TV show / comics / book series / film franchise / podcast as you. The fandom, whatever it may be, acts as the friendship glue and the source of much mutual excitement. You might only interact with them through one medium, like Twitter, conventions, or a book club. You may not share much in common outside of this niche interest, but that's OK! It feels pretty amazing to know people who love the same thing you do, and just as much as you do.

THE ENSEMBLE CAST

In a group, these are the friends you aren't incredibly close with, but you are still so glad they're around. Their company is joyous. You share meals, hobbies, interests, inside jokes, but you also don't hang out with them one-on-one or exchange deep secrets. And that's not a strike against anybody. Friendships do not have to be revealing or intimate to be important.

THE UNPAID INTERN

Friends help each other. Friends lend their time. But if one friend is always helping / giving their time / doing favors / running errands for the other, that's a power imbalance. Wallace from *Veronica Mars* comes to mind. He did so much work for Veronica in the beginning of the series that he should have been on the Mars Investigations payroll. This is a common pattern to fall into, and it's important to be aware of whether or not you are forcing any of your friends to be your personal assistant. Do you give help freely and gladly? If you don't, consider what it might mean to recover some of your time and energy.

YOUNGER SIBLING AND OLDER SIBLING

Some people want siblings (or additional siblings, or better siblings than the ones they have). Or they want to care for and mentor someone, or be taken care of and mentored themselves. Whatever the reason, lots of people have friendships with a siblinglike dynamic, particularly

What Do Good Friends
DO FOR EACH OTHER?

- The occasional annoying favor, like check your résumé for spelling errors, or help move that giant armoire to the alley when it's ninety-five degrees out

- Check on you proactively, especially in times of difficulty

- Happily introduce you to more people

- Treat your loved ones, pets, children, and family with courtesy, even if they aren't close themselves

- Celebrate or ignore your birthday, depending on what you prefer

- Laugh both with you and at you

- Tell you when your jokes are too mean

- Say nice things about you, even when you're not around

- Start a story by saying, "Remember when . . . ?"

- Commiserate with you when you complain about work, the person you're dating, or how hungover you are

- Dislike the same people you dislike, if only hypothetically

- Help you set up an online dating profile

- Help you delete an online dating profile

- Share recipes, books, board games, inside jokes, and their Netflix password

- Encourage you to do that thing you've been meaning to do, like run a marathon or take a martial arts class

- Not judge you when you decide you don't want to run a marathon or take a martial arts class

those with an age differential. Intergenerational friendships can be amazing. But the "older sibling" in this relationship needs to be wary of the power imbalances and cautious about babying or talking down to their friend. Adults should be treated as adults.

This isn't an all-inclusive list, but giving thought to the dynamics of your current friendships can be a meaningful exercise. You might sense real potential and start to build a bridge to someone—a stronger connection. Or you could decide to strike out and meet entirely new people. No matter what your circumstances are, we want you to have realistic yet high standards for friends. In fact, we demand it. You've got exactly one life ahead of you—as far as we know, anyway—and you deserve people who are kind and caring to you almost all of the time. (No one is kind all of the time.) As you begin this friendshipping journey, we give you complete permission to leave behind anyone who makes you feel anything but worthwhile.

WHERE TO MEET NEW FRIENDS

You might never feel totally prepared to meet new people. You probably won't leap out of bed one morning and yell: "Hello, world! I'm ready for you!" Unfortunately, you may have to force yourself to start before you feel ready. Because unless you're making friends on the internet (which is totally legitimate—more on this later), you'll have to leave your home to make friends. You'll have to go to new places, often by yourself, and talk to people. We're very sorry about this. But we're here to help! And, before you get started, know that there is no one-size-fits-all approach to meeting new people. Making friends as an adult is really challenging, and it's a challenge you can take on from many different angles.

START CLOSE TO HOME

Perhaps you already have a built-in resource, but you don't know it yet. We're talking about the friends and acquaintances you currently have in your life. These folks will naturally be invited to events that you aren't, and sometimes you can tag along. Tell your pal you are ready to meet new people and ask if they have any group hangouts on the horizon. Be clear about what you are looking for. Here are some scripts to get you thinking, but feel free to use your own words:

- *You doing anything fun in the next few weeks? If so, count me in—I'm up for meeting some new people.*
- *Next time you [play bar trivia / have a bonfire / go to a block party / host a movie night], I want to come, too, if that's cool! I had a blast last time and would love to see your nice friends again.*

USING YOUR WORDS

It can be really difficult to pick the right words to express exactly what you mean, especially when you're nervous or stressed. Throughout this book, we suggest "scripts" for you to borrow, like the ones above and on page 19. Unlike scripts for a movie or a play, these are not meant for you to memorize and say word-for-word. There's no director or line coach. These scripts are just guides for when you enter tricky territory. Remix 'em. Cut some adverbs. Add more cursing. Remove some cursing. And as you translate our words into your particular situation, be sure that you don't soften your meaning too, too much. Certainly, there are times to be flexible. But we want you to assertively, productively, and kindly state your needs, not whisper them into the void.

- *I'm thinking of finding a group to [go bowling / play strategy board games / start a book club]. Are you interested, and do you know anyone who would be down to join?*
- *I'm in the mood to meet some new folks. If you have any cool friends to introduce me to, I'm open!*
- *Friend, I've been thinking lately that I need to meet some new people and broaden my horizons. If you've got any group hangs on your social calendar over the next few months, please count me in.*

If you're close with this friend, then share your exact intentions and feelings to more aptly get your point across:

- *I need to [get out of the house more / have more fun / meet some new people / change up my social life / try something new]. I'd love to plan something fun for this weekend, but I don't really know who to invite. What if you did the inviting?*
- *Friend, I gotta tell ya, I've been feeling down lately and I could use some company. Want to help me on my quest to meet new people?*

Notice that you aren't being pushy or inviting yourself to a specific event, like a private dinner party. You're just making it known that you want something different in your social life and you would appreciate any invites thrown your way. You're telling the world that you are DTF: *Down to Friend.*

Dear Friendshipping,

I moved to a new city for my husband's job. His work keeps him very busy, and I'm finding myself with way too much time to spare as I search for my own employment. While I'm looking, I'd like to have some fun, too! Where do I even start?

You say that "having fun" is your goal, so let's explore that. Maybe you want a friend, but it could also be that you need to take yourself out to the movies, download a video game, get lost in a book series, or learn to juggle fruit. You can do these things on your own. Invest in yourself and your interests. You are fun company already! New friends will not always create immediate fun for you. If you're looking for someone to enter your life and dazzle you with a dozen new activities, you are looking for a camp counselor, not necessarily a friendship. Regardless, here's a place to start: Use the power of the internet to find events and volunteer opportunities near you. Put yourself in the right room.

GO SOMEWHERE (ANYWHERE!) BY YOURSELF

Some people find it blissful and freeing, but that's not the case for everyone. Marginalized people often have to add a whole extra step of care and research (*Will this place accommodate my mobility needs? How likely is it that I'll be hassled for my gender presentation? Will I be the only BIPOC there?*) before venturing out unaccompanied.

If you feel like you can do it safely and comfortably, going someplace alone is a good step toward friend-making. If you end up sitting next to a beer expert and having a great convo, that's a fun bonus. Or perhaps you're visiting the library alone. Go with the intention of borrowing three new-to-you cookbooks, and if you happen to talk to someone nearby about their family paella recipe, awesome. If you spot a flyer on the bulletin board advertising a free cooking class, even better. Essentially, we want you to put yourself in potentially social situations with non-social goals (teaching yourself something interesting, going somewhere new, furthering your hobbies) so you don't place enormous pressure on yourself to make new friends immediately. Here are some places where you can try this out:

THE LIBRARY. Workshops, clubs, readings, talks, game nights—the library is home to dozens of free activities that seem too good to be true, but are, in fact, true.

CAFÉS, COFFEE SHOPS, RESTAURANTS, OR BARS. You can become the newest regular (who treats and tips the staff well).

THE PARK DISTRICT OR CHAMBER OF COMMERCE. Some park districts offer public concerts and movie nights; chambers of commerce

 usually organize farmers markets, festivals, and art weeks. These organizations have widely differing levels of funding and activity based on where you live, but it's worth investigating! The best way to start is to look up [where you live] [park district/chamber of commerce].

WEBSITES THAT COORDINATE MEETUPS, LIKE MEETUP.COM. Heads up: We've heard both success stories and horror stories from sites like these. They work because everyone is there with a shared interest and goal of meeting people, but they're also coming at ya from the wild west of the internet. Set expectations accordingly.

GAME NIGHTS. Check out your local game or comic shop. The staff at some shops organize weekly or monthly events so you can try out all the newest arrivals.

CONVENTIONS THAT CELEBRATE A HOBBY. There are cons for nearly everything you can think of, including but not at all limited to video games, quilt-making, BDSM, gardening, sneakers, magicians, celebrity impersonators, vintage cars, retro toys, tattoos, and snack food. If you strike up a conversation, you'll have at least one thing to talk about.

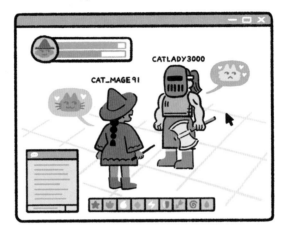

AMATEUR SPORTS LEAGUES. Soccer, softball, kickball, flag football—if you were a high school jock, this is your chance to relive the glory days. (There are usually low-key, less competitive leagues, too, if you're not super into the sport itself.) Just remember to be a good-natured and chill team-mate. Competitive activities can really bring out the aggression in people, unfortunately.

CLASSES. If you can afford it, consider signing up for a class and learning something new from a certified expert. People in large cities especially can find all kinds of workshops or boot camps in French cooking, calligraphy, metalworking, coding, whatever. Everyone there is new, like you, which evens the playing field. You already have something in common with the person beside you. Say hi and introduce yourself.

Whenever possible, we recommend selecting settings or events that have socializing already built in. We don't suggest trying to make new friends at, say, the gym. People are there to exercise. (Usually.) But if your gym hosts a charity event or holiday party, that would be the right time to say hi to new people.

FIND A WAY TO VOLUNTEER

Really, there's no sure-fire way for adults to meet potential friends, but another great avenue is volunteering. If that sounds like a cliché, then it's a cliché for a reason—it often works out well. Sign up to volunteer regularly at an organization, big or small, and we can almost guarantee that you will:

- Feel productive and accomplished, knowing you spent your time well
- Bond with interesting, like-minded people
- Practice empathy and patience
- Have something shiny and impressive to add to your résumé
- Learn about social issues (the kind of stuff you just can't absorb until you see it yourself)
- Hear fascinating stories
- Find even more avenues to meet people—organizations often host social gatherings and fundraisers, giving you more events to attend

How do you find the right volunteer gig for you? First, decide what kind of tasks you're up to doing. What do you like enough that you'd do it for free for a few hours a week or month? Perhaps it's organizing spreadsheets, designing flyers, or picking up trash outside. Search for an organization that aligns with your preferences and works with your schedule. It's totally OK to have strong opinions here! Figure out what tasks you hate doing, so you can avoid those as well as you can. Volunteer organizations benefit when you are dedicated and enthusiastic, not when you are dreading every second you have to be there.

When Jenn is looking for volunteer opportunities, she seeks places that don't need people to send emails or speak with the general public. She does not want to do either of those things. Sounds rude, she knows. But she does enough emailing and talking with people in her daily life. She wants to be away from a computer screen for once, and she doesn't particularly want to hear herself pontificate any more than she already does. That's why she volunteers at animal shelters whenever she can. Dogs don't give a shit. They don't even know what email is. (Must be nice.) Animals want affection, food, and exercise, and she is totally up for providing that. She also volunteers with an organization that mails books to women who are incarcerated. She selects books from the shelf and bundles packages to drop in the mail—it's quiet and soothing and doesn't dip into her limited well of energy. Trin, on the other hand, works from home full-time, so her well of energy is different: She enjoys canvassing door-to-door, speaking with people, and being part of an active crowd, like at a protest or rally.

Once you've got an idea of what you like to do. find an organization that you are excited about and let that energy carry you out your front door. Queer spaces, animal adoption centers, food banks, blood drives, clothing drives, book drives, theaters, libraries, crisis centers, clinics, hospitals—so many orgs could use your commitment and passion. You could walk dogs who need fresh air, stock shelves at a food pantry, pull weeds in a community garden, tutor kids after school. You could teach English to immigrants who want to learn. You could volunteer for a local political campaign. (Political staffers tell us that volunteering for a local election is the best use of our time when getting douchebags out of office.) You might collect signatures, knock on doors, phone bank, ask for donations. Fixing our broken world isn't solely your responsibility, of course, and if you need your volunteer work to be low intensity, that's OK, too. But it may be worth stepping beyond your comfort zone.

When you find an organization you like, sign up through the official channels that are offered. You will often have to go through an orientation session or two to learn the ropes. After that, you have an order of operations. Socializing is not the priority. Your first priority is learning how to do your volunteer work safely and effectively. You are there to help by giving your time and attention, which is so kind of you, and worth taking seriously. But you can make friends *as* you work, not in spite of the work. In fact, it's often easier to hold a conversation while you are busy doing something—it takes the pressure off of you to be entertaining or deliver a perfectly timed anecdote. Observe the people who have worked there longer than you have and take cues from them on when it's OK to chat and relax. And before you get all chatty, assume there is another task to be done. There basically always is. Charity organizations are notoriously understaffed.

Just FYI, there *are* a couple downsides to trying to meet people this way: You will not necessarily see the same faces every time you volunteer, making it difficult to form connections with people. (No doubt you'll have to reintroduce yourself a few times.) Even if you volunteer often, some people only volunteer once a month. Others will put in their hours, like, three times a year. Some volunteers will show up once and never return. And the work will not be glamorous. The people in charge will be overworked and stressed. It will not be as exciting as it is in movies, with an uplifting sunny soundtrack and awed children hugging you after you do something incredible and impossible, like lifting the last wooden frame to finish building a house. But even if you make no friends at all, you're practicing social skills, gaining life experience, finding new stories to tell, and making the world one iota less sucky.

HARNESS THE POWER OF THE WORLD WIDE WEB

The year 2020 saw a pandemic sweep over the world, one that forced everyone to stay at least six feet apart. We all had to learn how to socialize without hanging out in person, using tools like video chat and online board games. But you don't have to use the internet just to maintain your relationships. You can use it to make entirely *new* friends! If that sounds downright weird to you: yeah, OK, that's fair. This may not be how you personally use the internet. But it's truly not strange to make online friends because we live in the age of technology. In the Victorian era, private messages were exchanged through the arrangement of flowers and plants. (Seriously. Google "language of flowers" sometime.) Elizabeth Barrett and Robert Browning exchanged letters before ever meeting. See, we all work with the tools we have, and right now, those tools are online.

What is it that you are most interested in? Crafting birdhouses? Crafting a skincare routine? Crafting a fantasy story? The internet hosts crowds of people ready to dissect and discuss whatever it is you're most excited about, and is especially helpful for those who are physically or more socially isolated. Jenn made friends online as a teenager through LiveJournal and Neopets (seriously). She searched for what she was obsessed with at the time—Kingdom Hearts, Death Cab for Cutie, and Orlando Bloom—and found posts that made her gasp in recognition and inspired her to leave comments like, "OMG, whut, I love Legolas, too! Want to add me on LiveJournal?!" LiveJournal was a tremendous part of Jenn's life—she posted long, self-indulgent missives and then gave people access to the journal as she got to know them. The internet brought fellow dorks right to her living room, and she's still friends with lots of these people today. (Admittedly, their interests haven't really changed that much.)

Of course, the internet, just like life outside of it, is crowded with assholes. Assholes really shine on the internet because they don't have to use their true identities and can behave horribly without much consequence. In order to find the nice, non-creepy people within a community, let's talk etiquette. Imagine that everyone online is hanging out in a huge metaphorical public park. In a public park, you would not:

- Scream insults at people nearby (or maybe you would, but we hope not)
- Crouch in the bushes and leer
- Ask strangers personal questions, like if they have a boyfriend, or where they live
- Force your way into a two-person conversation
- Follow around one person and comment critically on everything they are wearing, saying, or doing

But perhaps you *would* say hello to someone you very clearly had something in common with. If somebody in the park was wearing a shirt that said I LOVE TO READ ADVICE BOOKS ABOUT FRIENDSHIP, TALK TO ME ABOUT THEM ANYTIME! you might offer a friendly hello and a relevant story, and then you would move on or maybe grab their email address to chat more later. If someone else held a sign that said I LIVE FOR LATE '90s ROCK MUSIC! you would rush over and high-five them and offer your Twitter handle because it's @late90smusiclover420. But if it was your very first day in the park and you didn't find anyone with whom you had things in common, you probably would not say hi to anyone at all! You would simply try not to get lost in the park. Did that metaphor get out of hand? We are just encouraging you to wait a second before you

Dear Friendshipping,

I've got plans to meet up with someone I know through Twitter. We have lots in common, share the same sense of humor, and email all the time, so I feel like it'll go great. What do I need to know before we meet in person?

Before you meet up, mentally picture many different outcomes. We hope this goes great, and it certainly could, but you are still transitioning into a new phase of your friendship with this person. Manage your expectations. It's not that you are "finally" meeting this person; you do know them—but a version of them. Now you are meeting another version, and it might feel very strange. Perhaps they smell weird. Or they aren't as witty as they are via email. Or maybe they're so cool and suave IRL that you feel too intimidated to act like yourself. Be ready for a few surprises.

get all keyboard-happy. Spend time being observant before talking to people and sharing all of your genius opinions. Many social media platforms won't let you post for a full twenty-four hours after you sign up, and that is your chance to read the room. Wait until you feel confident that you have an obvious tie to a person—they work in your industry, you both homebrew kombucha—and use that as your pathway to saying hello.

And remember, a friendship doesn't have to check certain boxes in order to be significant—internet friends are indeed real friends. It can be a real boon to not have to think about your posture, makeup, or bad breath and just connect with a person without the anxiety of face-to-face interaction. Trin's friendships with the people in her old *World of Warcraft* guild were formative in her college years, which were otherwise pretty miserable. Becoming a better paladin was a confidence booster, and it was fun to play alongside respected peers (albeit the digital fantasy avatars of those respected peers). It's been ten years and Trin is still in touch with an old dungeon buddy (who happens to go by "McSprinkles").

In very special and fortunate circumstances, an internet friend *can* cross the bridge to an in-person friend. But you do not have to make this happen if what you're doing works well and you're both happy.

HOW TO MAKE THE FIRST FRIEND MOVE

Small talk has this negative reputation for being boring and shallow, but it's an essential part of meeting someone new and getting to know them better. It gives you a crucial opportunity to read someone's cues: if they're too distracted to talk, how familiar they are with the subject you're discussing, if they would prefer to be alone. Small talk with a stranger does not mean that you made a new friend—you just increase your chances of finding cool people you like when you engage in basic conversations. To excel at small talk, you don't need to be naturally charming or a public speaker with loads of experience. Small talk is a skill, and one that you can practice.

MEETING IN PERSON

Making the leap from online to in-person friends is something that all parties must consent to enthusiastically. People who are statistically more likely to be victims of violence—for example, because of their gender or their race—are particularly wary when it comes to meeting friends from the internet in person. If you decide to do it, here's what to keep in mind:

OBVIOUSLY, BE SAFE ABOUT IT. Even if you know this person really well online, including their full name and what their face looks like, still hold fast to the basic guidelines: Don't give out your exact address, always meet in a public setting, and be sure to tell another person where you'll be and how long you'll be there. (By the way, young people reading this: Don't do online meetups if you aren't a legal adult.)

ESTABLISH TIME LIMITS BEFOREHAND. "Let's meet for coffee for an hour" or "I'll have to run out around 8:00 p.m., but I would love to meet at the bookstore at 6:30!" This encounter could go beautifully, but if not, you don't want to be stuck in an unbearably awkward situation forever.

DON'T GO FOR THE HUG. Not everyone likes hugs. Not everyone likes hugs! Do not assume that your internet friend (or anyone!) is OK with being embraced. When you first meet someone, go for the handshake. Or just say "So awesome to see you! Would you prefer a hug or a high-five?" Or "You cool with hugs or nah?"

BE FORGIVING. You may find that you don't gel as well with your internet bud in person. Maybe you both communicate better when you're able to edit yourselves, like through email. This is a good time to be more forgiving of mild social errors. Give your friend—and yourself—a little extra room to make those awkward-but-ultimately-harmless kinds of mistakes.

STEP 1: DISCOVER YOUR STORIES.

Dr. John Antonakis, a professor of organizational behavior at the University of Lausanne in Switzerland, says that charisma is essentially the ability to tell a story. He said the most charismatic people in a room have anecdotes ready to share and energetic body language to match. As you're reading this, you may think that you don't have a single interesting story, but that's not true. You totally do. You've broken rules or taken risks. You've had experiences that were hilarious or romantic or spooky or dangerous or embarrassing or coincidental. You don't need to have a revolving repertoire of hilarious jokes, a history of sexy bank heists, or a lucrative movie deal to be worthy of conversation. You don't have to be entertaining or "impressive" (what does that even mean, anyway?) to share parts of yourself with others. Your stories are in your brain, just waiting for you to unbury and share them. If you're having trouble coming up with personal anecdotes, here are a few suggestions to spark your creativity:

EXAMINE YOUR ROUTINE. Dig a little deeper into what feels ordinary to you, but might surprise someone else. What's on your mind during your commute? What are you reading or listening to? What have you been cooking lately? What are you watching? Why?

START WITH A STRONG EMOTION. When's the last time you felt shocked? How about brave? Triumphant? Delighted? Maybe you saved your elderly neighbor from an internet scam, spotted a celebrity at the airport last week, or saw a dog do the funniest thing at the park.

LOOK BACK ON AN EVENT. Visual aids will help you remember the stories that you've lived. Do you have memorable emails or text messages you can look through? What about photos? Scrapbooks? Journals? Yearbooks? Keepsakes? Even social media could help with this.

LISTEN TO OTHERS WITH INTENTION. Collect and share the stories you hear. Give credit when it's due and don't share personal info, but something like, "My coworker told me her uncle proposed to his girlfriend in the middle of a wedding reception. Can you imagine how awkward that must have been?" is definitely worth the retell.

CONVERSATION STARTERS

- We haven't met before, have we? I'm Subi, by the way. My pronouns are she/her.

- Tell me about you!

- What are your favorite [restaurants / record stores / coffee shops / bookstores / parks / trails / jogging routes] around here?

- How did you meet the host?

- I'm looking for some new reading material. Picked up any good books lately?

- Have you ever met a celebrity?

- How do you like to spend your free time?

- What's the last TV show you loved?

STEP 2: FOLLOW THE GUIDELINES.

Maybe you've never felt confident making small talk. Maybe you're just out of practice and could use a refresher course. First, remind yourself that not every single conversation must dazzle and amaze. That's a lot of pressure on yourself. Most convos will be uneventful, and that's enough! If you're nervous, take a moment to inhale and exhale slooowly before you approach anybody. You're more likely to say something regrettable or act on your crappy ingrained biases if you feel stressed. Mellow your expectations and follow these guidelines for making small talk that is pleasant, polite, and engaging:

TAKE YOUR AUDIENCE, THE SETTING, AND THE MOOD INTO ACCOUNT.
Is it too crowded and noisy to say much more than hello? Does the general mood feel off or low energy, as if someone just received bad news? Are other people talking, too, or is the room completely silent and full of people reading quietly?

DO A LITTLE BRAINSTORMING. Before a social event, take time to brainstorm some safe and lightconvo topics (see Step 1). This mental exercise will a) make you realize how interesting you are, and b) prepare you to talk about yourself.

ASK POLITE QUESTIONS AND SHARE ABOUT YOURSELF IN RETURN.
These questions might depend on the situation: If you're talking to a coworker, maybe you start off with, "I've worked in this building for years; how about you?" If it's a friend of a friend, perhaps you say, "I love your boots! I need a new pair for hiking this weekend; where did you get those?"

TRUST YOUR INTERNAL PERSONAL FILTER. Not every thought you have needs to be shared with the class. Got a feeling that you shouldn't say something out loud? Listen to it. You can always say something at a different time, but you can never *unsay* it. Here's an example of awful small talk: An acquaintance once approached Jenn and asked how long she had been shaving her arm hair.

TAKE NOTE OF SILENT/SUBTLE CUES. At best, unwanted small talk is an interruption. At worst, it's harassment. But most people don't feel empowered to come out and say, "You know, I could use some time in my own head right now. I'm sorry, but I actually would prefer to not make conversation." Instead, we tend to excuse ourselves when we don't want to make small talk with a "Soft No." It can look like glancing toward the door, shifting away, or saying, "It was nice talking with you." It may seem disingenuous when you're on the receiving end, but everyone does this from time to time as an instinctual attempt to be polite, accommodating, and not make an uncomfortable situation even more awkward with a confrontation.

Is the person you're speaking with fiddling with their phone, wearing headphones, or looking around the room instead of at your face? Are they settling in to chat longer, or are they digging in their backpack for their book? Are you involved in the conversation, or are you grilling a stranger with questions? Or, quite simply, are they on their way toward the door? If you're getting only one-word answers and this person is edging away from you, that's a Soft No. Kindly move on.

Allegedly, when Ringo Starr greets legions of fans, he's quite friendly but never stops moving. Very smart of him! He's a living example of the Soft No. Such is life for a Beatle. Here are examples of the Soft No in more routine situations:

MILA: It seems like we always run into each other for a 2:00 p.m. coffee break! Hi, I'm Mila. I go by they/them pronouns.
STEVEN: Nice to meet you, I'm Steven. He/him pronouns. Enjoy your coffee!

MILA: We meet again at 2:00 p.m.! I'm Mila, they/them.
STEVEN: Good running into ya! See you again tomorrow!

In those examples, Steven returns the greeting from Maya, but he signals the end of the conversation. And notice that he's not unfriendly or impolite in the slightest. Conversely, here are examples of "Yes, Let's Keep Chattin'" responses.

MILA: I always see you in here and thought I would say hello! I'm Mila, they/them.

STEVEN: Nice to meet you, I'm Steven. He/him. How's your day going?

MILA: I'm Mila. I use they/them. Man, Tuesdays, am I right?

STEVEN: Seriously. I had to flee my cubicle before I stapled my hand to my desk. I'm Steven, by the way. He/him.

STEP 3: KEEP IT LIGHT

It's called small talk for a reason—you shouldn't go digging around for the big stuff yet. When you meet someone, stick to questions and topics that skim the surface, like, "Have you lived in Chicago long?" or "Where did you get those incredible espadrilles?" Avoid conversations that start with "Do you believe in life after death?" or "How did you get that scar?" or "When was the last time you cried?" Keep the conversation light, and hold back on sharing the stories of, say, your childhood trauma. Even if *you* don't mind sharing darker stories, consider your impact and how others may feel; you could accidentally trigger an upsetting memory for someone else.

Of course, there are exceptions here. Maybe you are sitting around a cozy bonfire and everyone is sharing their heavier stuff. It does happen, and it can be cathartic to get lost in a bottle of wine and get real with people. Savor those rare moments, but don't expect them to happen on command.

We also caution you against making extended small talk with people who are on the clock and working, like your barista, flight attendant, or customer service representative. "Hi, how are you today?" and "Did you have a good weekend?" are courteous pleasantries. This is not an opportunity for you to dish about your life and steal time from

PRONOUN ETIQUETTE

Here's a quick grammar lesson: Pronouns replace nouns and often work as an expression of gender (she, he, her, him, they, them, and many more). Here's a quick human decency lesson: When you use someone's pronouns properly, you are showing respect by treating this person as a person. When someone tells you the pronouns they use ("Hi, nice to meet you, I'm Lin, and my pronouns are they/them"), you should:

USE THEIR PRONOUNS FROM THAT POINT FORWARD. If this is hard for you to do, practice! Say to yourself *This is my new friend Lin, they're an attorney, they live next door, they just adopted a dog . . .* Mentally place pronouns in the same category as someone's name. It is both courteous and essential to know and correctly pronounce someone's name, right? Same with pronouns.

SHARE YOURS IN TURN, IF IT FEELS SAFE AND RIGHT FOR YOU TO DO SO. "I'm Shane. My pronouns are he/him." "Got it, thanks. Mine are she/her." And when you can, share your pronouns first. Especially if you are cis! (Cis people often say, "He, she, they—call me whatever you like, it doesn't matter!" in an attempt to be welcoming, but this is trivializing and belittling to non-cis people.) Sharing your pronouns first is especially great to do group settings. If you've got a name tag,

people who are paid to be polite. Don't do the thing where you lean on the counter and get comfortable, as if you're planning to camp out and stay awhile. Do not stay awhile. (Of course you can have a conversation with, say, your cab/ride-share driver, but ensure that you are getting consistent social cues that signal they're enthusiastic to talk. Remember that they can't escape unless they throw themselves from a moving car.)

add your pronouns to it, even if you think your pronouns should be "obvious." This is particularly important if you've got some kind of authority, like you're the host of the party or the dungeon master of a DnD campaign. You're establishing a welcoming and accepting tone.

APOLOGIZE QUICKLY IF YOU MAKE A MISTAKE. If you slip up and use the wrong pronouns (this does happen, but you are not a monster), make a short apology in the moment, correct yourself without fuss, and move on. You don't need to make an emotional display out of your error. Just do better in the future. (And if you witness other people get your friends' pronouns wrong, it's cool to correct them. No need to make a scene, but a quick and firm, "You mean 'she,'" can be very meaningful and helpful.)

You should not:

DISAGREE, ARGUE, DEBATE, OR ASK A TON OF FOLLOW-UP QUESTIONS. Kindly accept the information you are given. If you're confused, go online to do research; be your own teacher.

ARGUE ABOUT GRAMMAR. "They" can be a singular pronoun. It's in the dictionary this way. Maybe it's not easy to start using they/them pronouns for the first time in your life, but your grammatical discomfort is much less important than someone else's existential discomfort.

STEP 4: BE MINDFUL OF PERSONAL SPACE

We don't want you to overthink every single interaction, but we do have to mention this: physical contact. Be aware of the amount of distance you are or are not giving people, and how your unconscious biases may be affecting your body language. (For example, white people have a horrible habit of touching Black women's hair.) Perhaps you're a touchy-feely type who loves to give and receive platonic physical affection. That is totally normal and does not make you a big creep. It's OK to give a friend a quick hug, an amicable pat on the shoulder, or a little elbow nudge. These are friendly gestures that don't typically indicate sexual or romantic interest. But if you enjoy physical human contact, you have some special responsibilities: You ought to pay attention to how often you are being touchy, if and when these gestures may be unwanted, and if you are giving someone *too much* of your physical attention. When you first meet someone, you just don't know how comfortable they are with this stuff unless you ask. Even if you have known someone for a long time, you may not know their comfort level in the moment. So if you have doubts, no touching. Remember, too, that boundaries are subject to change at any time. Perhaps your friend once enjoyed an embrace when you said hello, but now they prefer to shake hands instead of hugging. Respect the change.

STEP 5: COMPLIMENTS > COMPLAINTS

There *is* one type of small talk we'd generally like you to avoid: group complaining. Maybe you recognize this scenario: You're with people you don't know very well and you're unsure of what to say, so you default to complaining about something around you. And, honestly, sometimes it's fine if everyone is ragging on the crappy weather outside or a rival sports team. But the difference between that and everyone talking about how the music is off-key or the guacamole is gross is that someone put time and effort into making the latter things happen! What if you hurt someone's feelings? What if someone worked really hard on that gross guac?! And besides, the conversation will likely run out of steam. In either scenario, you aren't learning about anyone, nor are you sharing about yourself, which are the two most basic ways to make a connection.

CONVERSATION ENDERS

- *What do your tattoos mean?* (Believe it or not, this is a very personal question. And don't ask if you can touch anyone's tattoos or see more of the ones that are hidden under clothing.)

- *Where are you from? No, like, originally, where are you from?*

- *Where are your parents from?* (This line of question is racist, intrusive, and aggravating.)

- *Can I get you a drink? Oh, you don't drink? Why? What happened?* (Doesn't matter why someone doesn't drink alcohol, it's not your business.)

Instead, get in the habit of giving compliments. There's no need to make up compliments for the sake of conversation—it's obvious when you're being insincere—but if you earnestly think a nice thing about somebody, say that nice thing out loud! Especially if you can do it in one or two sentences. (Your compliment is intended to make someone feel noticed in a positive way; it's not for you to shine a beaming spotlight on their face and deliver your best Oscar-worthy gushing speech.) Some examples of acceptable and friendly compliments:

- *It was really nice meeting you tonight! I'm glad we got to talk.*
- *You're such a friendly host. Thanks for making me feel welcome here.*
- *This playlist is incredible. You have good taste in music.*
- *You are brightening up the room!*
- *Did you make this granola? It rocks my ass off.*

Proceed with caution when you are complimenting someone's looks. You can safely offer compliments about appearance, but only if you internalize this rule first: *Thou shall not make unsolicited remarks about anyone's body.* That includes comments like this:

- *Did you lose a bunch of weight? You look so hot now!*
- *Wow, do you work out? It shows.*
- *Most women wear way too much makeup, but you're naturally beautiful.*

Even if well-intended, these are not nice things to say. Your intentions don't really matter; only you know your intentions. What matters the most is the harm you could cause this person or anyone who happens to be listening. If your friend is suddenly "hot" after weight loss (which is not always a happy or healthy event), what are you saying about their body before, and what are you saying about everyone else? Why trash on others just to tell your friend that she looks nice?

Comments like these also presume that there is one "look" that everyone should aspire to, which isn't true. Plus, words like "hot" can indicate sexual interest and can make a friend feel confused or uncomfortable. Yikes!

The wiser and kinder choice: If you want to compliment someone's looks, say something nice about an active choice they made. Compliment the *decision* they made to wear those high-heeled boots or that patterned tie, without mentioning a specific body part. Highlight their great taste or their eye for style. *Those shoes are next-level* is so much better than *You have such sexy feet!* You've pointed to their fashion acumen and—bonus!—you left the conversation open to discuss trending footwear.

STEP 6: FORGIVE YOUR FUTURE SELF

Finally, know that at some point you *will* say something wrong or embarrassing or awkward, even when you are making every effort to be kind and funny. You're human, and mistakes are inevitable. And hey, sometimes those mistakes make delightful anecdotes later on. One time a handsome stranger in a Starbucks told Trin's friend standing near her that she was beautiful. Trin replied, "Thank you." The thing is, everyone has moments like these. Forgive yourself for them.

But what if this all goes very badly? We just told you to get out of your house, try new things, and talk to people, all of which are very scary. Now we are giving you permission to do the utterly unthinkable: You can leave! You are officially authorized to exit any conversation,

Dear Friendshipping,

I'd like to know what sort of things I can do to encourage continued friendship with people I meet. Any ideas?

Not every person you chat with will become your friend. Many people you meet you will never see again. That's OK! You are flexing your socializing muscles. But when you meet someone you can and do want to see again, be as clear as possible that you're down for real, actual friendship. It's such a delicate (but doable) dance of not overwhelming them while being friendly and inviting. It's like luring a stray cat to your house. You must offer the treat of friendship with an open palm: "This piece of deli meat is here for you to take, if you want it. I present no danger, and I will not advance." Or, in other words: "I feel like we really hit it off! Any interest in getting a bite to eat after class next week?"

place, or event, at any time. One of the few upsides of making friends as an adult is that you are in charge of yourself. Isn't that kind of great? You can freely come to the realization that, actually, volunteering for local blood drives is a great thing, but it just isn't right for your abilities or schedule, and you can kindly remove yourself from the volunteer mailing list. No harm done. If you're at a party and feeling listless, bored, or miserable, you can leave as soon as you're ready. If you're in a social situation and you're uncomfortable—you're exhausted, tense, hungry—you are not really setting yourself up for success in making new friends anyway.

In general, you oughta be courteous and polite when you make your exit, unless of course the people involved do not deserve that. For those particular moments, feel free to fantasize about using these ideas:

- *I would rather burn the roof of my mouth on hot soup than spend another minute at this party.*
- *There are so many kind and considerate people in the world, and you are not one of them.*
- *Amazing, relaxing, fun, awesome—these are not words I would use to describe my time here.*
- *What a waking nightmare! I hope we never cross paths again.*
- *Wrestling a mountain lion would be more enjoyable than listening to you speak. I'm going to go find one.*
- *We thought my coming here would be a good idea. We were both wrong.*
- *To be honest, I will probably never speak with you again. Have a nice life!*

But, naturally, you want to leave most situations politely. Here are some scripts that you can use to announce your graceful exit:

- *I've got some stuff I need to go take care of, so I'm heading out now. I wanted to say thanks for having me.*
- *Yes, the rumors are true. I really am leaving now.*
- *Hey, it was great talking with you. I'm going to go say hi to a few more folks. Catch you later?*
- *I'm going to slip out, but thanks for the chat! I appreciated your in-depth analysis of all Michael Bay's movies.*
- *I'm going to head out in about five minutes, so I am beginning my goodbye tour.*

If you want to talk to this person more or see them again, definitely say so! You can even mention follow-up plans:

- *Thanks for letting me stop by. This was really fun, and I loved getting to know everyone here. Invite me to the next group thing, please!*
- *I need to go home to recharge my social battery now. Thanks for inviting me out. Let's do this again soon, yeah?*
- *I'm going to head out now, but keep me cc'd on all your future group invites!*
- *Can I send you an email next week about taking our kids to the zoo? Because I love that idea!*

It's also totally acceptable to offer a little white lie if you need to escape an event or convo quickly ("I'm going back inside to grab a refill," or "I have to head home now, it's my turn to relieve my partner of toddler duty," or "Oops, gotta run to a client dinner"). And just because things didn't turn out as well as you hoped or you reached your limit for social interaction doesn't mean that you should never attend another party or volunteer somewhere ever again. We aren't telling you to give up. Just the opposite, really: You oughta try again, but under different circumstances. Think of the new social life you're building as an ongoing science experiment in which you are getting to know yourself. When you try new things, you are gathering data. Would you have had more fun at the party if you'd brought someone along with you? If the host had been more hosty and introduced you to people? Maybe coming straight from work made you sleepy, or next time you can experiment with having less (or more!) beer. These aren't tremendous errors—you are simply noticing what you can change for next time. Even if you felt incredibly anxious speaking out loud at the book club meeting, you put yourself out there, and you learned that you'll never go to Linda's condo to discuss science fiction ever again because it's not your thing. That's valuable information. So go easy on yourself here. You're putting in the effort. You're socializing! Going somewhere new, talking to someone you haven't spoken with before—these are victories worth

Professional Small Talk
AKA NETWORKING

Networking can feel a little gross, like you are being friendly to people because you might want something from them. "What can this person do for me professionally?" is the question that colors your interactions. But networking really is useful. People from underrepresented  groups tend to rely on networking and mentorship since they are typically less likely to be hired and promoted.

Here are a few prompts to get you started (remember to share about yourself, too):

- *What kind of projects are you working on at the moment?*

- *How'd you get your start in the industry?*

- *What's your role at your company?*

- *What's your day-to-day like?*

- *What's your favorite thing you've worked on this year?*

- *Is this your first time at the conference, or are you a seasoned veteran?*

- *What keeps you coming back each year?*

- *What's the best [booth / talk / vendor / presentation] you've seen so far?*

- *I've been talking about work for three days straight, so, new topic! What's the last movie you saw in theaters?*

- *What's on your reading list?*

- *I've got a long flight home. What [podcast / music / lecture] should I listen to?*

- *What's the last TV show you binged?*

celebrating. Friendship doesn't happen overnight or with the snap of a finger. Stay hopeful, stay mindful. You've already done the brave thing and made the first step. Small steps forward are steps forward.

REKINDLING AN OLD FRIENDSHIP FLAME

Perhaps you recently happened across your long-lost best friend from elementary school on social media. At a glance, they don't seem horrible. Maybe you've still got some shared opinions and interests. Does this mean you should reach out? Well, this person is a stranger now—a stranger with whom you presumably still have a few things in common. Friendships have formed over less! So you can try to get in touch, and it *can* go well, but keep your expectations low and reasonable. There's a possibility that it will go poorly and that you will feel rejected by your best friend from elementary school. Is that possibility OK with you? Or would you rather remember this friendship fondly and not sully it by attempting to tack on a sequel?

You will enter and leave many friendships throughout your life, usually without much fanfare. People drift apart, and it's often nobody's fault. It's sometimes even for the best! You might miss old friends, you might not—maybe you simply look back with affection and have no desire to catch up. You don't *have* to want old friends back and light a candle in church for them every week and pray to the patron saint of friendship (St. John the Apostle,

FYI). You can simply accept that you're doing fine without them, and likewise they are doing fine without you. Relationships don't have to be permanent to be important. We can have people who enter our lives

Making the
TOUGH DECISIONS

Should I apologize to someone I ghosted years ago? Can I ask to borrow money from a friend? Is it too weird to ask my academic advisor to hang out? If you are feeling stuck on a decision, the first thing to do is picture an array of outcomes. Know the potential risks and the rewards. Of course, this is difficult because we're not working with numbers here. You're never going to know if there's a 73 percent chance of an awkward moment. It's more like you have to carry the emotional weight of all possibilities in your heart and decide what load seems lightest for you to bear. Ask yourself:

- *Ideally, what do I want to happen?*

- *What option will bring me the most peace?*

- *What is the worst-case scenario? Is it something that I could live with?*

Here's an example that includes weighing the risks, predicting the outcomes, and then estimating how those outcomes will make you feel:

Chanelle wants to reconnect with her childhood friend Olly, but she's hesitating because based on his social media profiles, he seems like he's become a bit of a jerk. She decides that she'd rather keep the happy memories intact than meet up and be disappointed in how he's changed.

Or: *Chanelle wants to reconnect with her childhood friend Olly, even though it's been a long time, and he's definitely different now. She decides to invite him for a coffee and catch up. If they don't get along, it'll be a shame, but it's not the end of the world. They'll always have their fun memories.*

Like Chanelle, you can and should focus on what's best for you in any tricky situation. And remember: You can do difficult things. You can survive awkward moments. In fact, you already have.

as "buds from college" or "summer camp friends." It's like traveling—a weekend away in a new city is worth your time, even if you don't bring everything you own and put a down payment on a house while you're there. Still, there may come a time when you do want to reconnect with someone from your past. It's a delicate process, but it's possible. Here's how to do it appropriately:

DON'T OVERREACH. Use the means at your immediate disposal to make contact in a no-pressure kind of way. If you have their email address, go ahead and email them. If it bounces back, don't dig around the internet until you locate their outdated blog and send them an anonymous message saying that you want to get in touch. If you have to go through a series of steps to reach out, then you shouldn't reach out. Err on the side of caution in this case. Remember that when you reach out, you're going to surprise this person.

Dear Friendshipping,

I saw through social media that a coworker I was close with years and years ago recently moved to my city. How do I reboot a friendship from yesteryear?

Go ahead and reach out! If they moved very recently, they might need a little time to unpack and adjust before they start taking visitors. So propose something like meeting up for lunch, or showing them around your favorite places in the city. But know this: Your new friendship could be a shot-for-shot remake of the original, as if barely any time has passed since you've seen each other. But maybe not! It could be more of a spiritual successor, only loosely inspired by the franchise. This person has had "years and years" of life away from you, so be ready to ask questions and learn who they've now become.

CONTACT THEM ONCE, THEN WAIT. Send one polite email or short message on social media. If they don't reciprocate, focus your energy on other friends.

DON'T EXPECT AN IMMEDIATE REUNION. It might take a few weeks of email exchanges for you to feel comfortable becoming friends again (if that even happens!).

REMEMBER THAT INTERNET FRIENDSHIPS COUNT, TOO. There's no reason why "Your Friend from Junior High" can't turn into "Your Friend You Exchange Emails With." Internet friendships are a low-energy way to keep in touch, but they are still friendships.

Even if you were once very close friends, there are so many completely harmless reasons why you might not hear back from them. For example:

THEY DON'T HAVE THE TIME OR BANDWIDTH. This is incredibly likely. Your old friend might not be able to reignite the friendship because of other responsibilities, including but not limited to school, raising children, wedding planning, divorce planning, bills, travel, and job changes. Maybe they meant to respond, but just forgot. Maybe there's an internet outage in their town. Even if they post nothing but pictures of themselves laughing and drinking wine with their attractive spouse, that's only a fleeting, microscopic glimpse into their life. They don't always live like that, and that doesn't mean they have extra energy or time to give to you. Not getting a response doesn't mean your old friendship was not important or meaningful to them.

THE PAST HURTS. It's not that they don't treasure the good times with you, but perhaps they don't look back fondly on their high school years and would rather move away from them completely. You could represent a part of their past they wish to leave decidedly in the past. An old friend of Jenn's once sent her a message on Facebook, and it brought on such a rush of weird memories that she not only immediately closed Facebook, but snapped her laptop shut and left the room. Calm and collected as usual!

THEY DIDN'T SEE THE MESSAGE. You know this is possible. Hasn't this happened to you before? It could be that they never check their email (can you imagine?) or don't use social media anymore.

If you do manage to hold a few fun and light conversations and you'd like to try hanging out in person, you can issue an invitation. Do this just once, with specific plans (and see page 52 for more ways to initiate friend hangs):

- *Hi again! I was wondering if you'd like to get coffee this weekend and catch up. Saturday afternoon and Sunday morning are good for me. Let me know what works for you. And bring pictures of that new baby!*
- *A bunch of us from the office are going to go see a Metallica tribute band this Friday. I thought that might interest you. Let me know if you plan to make it. I would love to grab a drink or sing loudly near you.*

If you end up hanging out with your old bud, you'll have to refriend them. You are not the same people you were in high school (thankfully) or whenever it was that you were close, so remember to:

TREAT THIS PERSON LIKE A NEW PAL. You have a jumping-off point— you've got an overlapping history—but it's still a new friendship. And new friendships are awkward! Take some time to reminisce about your shared past, but remember to ask questions about this person's here and now. If you aren't genuinely interested in their new life and you're just here for nostalgia, this probably isn't worth pursuing much further.

AVOID GUILT TRIPS. Don't make the other person feel bad for being gone a while. Start with a clean slate. Avoid "Where have you been?" or "How come I've never heard from you?" Try "I'd love to hear about your life!" or "I'm excited to learn what you've been up to."

TALK ABOUT YOUR LIFE, TOO. You'll only know if you're still compatible if you offer bits of your true self. You are more than just your job, or your homework, or your kid, or your daily chores. Tell your friend who you are now.

This all might work beautifully, or it could immediately hit a dead end. Be prepared for either outcome. It can be painful when people reject your offer to reconnect, but you have not actually lost anything.

On the other side of this, you are not making an unkind decision if someone contacts you and you simply don't want to reconnect. You are not behaving incorrectly by having preferences and deciding whom to give time to. People will come and go; this is, quite simply, a refrain of adulthood. Your lifetime of experiences and your understanding of the world can only grow and change with each hurt and joy you live through. Honor the time you spent in your old friendships by learning from them and actively using those lessons in your new connections.

HOW TO INVITE SOMEONE TO HANG

Say you've met someone you like at a PTA meeting. You've had a dozen friendly conversations, they seem to like you back, and you want to hang outside of the meeting. This is a great time to issue an invitation. Treat it like the casual, no-pressure, no-strings-attached event that it is—you're not proposing friend-marriage for life. You're trying something new and different for you, and that's valuable regardless of the outcome. Here's how to extend an invitation:

HAVE A SPECIFIC EVENT IN MIND. "Let's get coffee sometime" is too vague to be effective. "Do you want to get tacos from the place around the corner after our meeting next Wednesday?" is a thought-out plan. If you want to make it crystal clear you are asking this person to hang as a friend and *not* asking them out on a date, include more people: "I'm trying to get a group together to see that new pottery exhibit at the museum." Or "My wife and I are going to a movie on Saturday. We have room in our car for more if you are interested." Or "My roommate and I are making plans to hit up the apple orchard. Do you want to come with us? You can bring your kids, too."

PLACE YOUR FOCUS ON THE EVENT OR THE HOBBY. Find something that you would like to do even if the other person can't attend. "I've heard this documentary on the history of the pencil eraser is a thrill ride. I'm going to see it on Saturday. You interested in joining?" Or "The noodle place across the street has an amazing lunch deal I'm going to try—any interest in finishing our meeting over there?"

IT'S OK TO ACKNOWLEDGE THE WEIRDNESS. Making friends as a grown-up is not easy. You can point that out: "I fully do not want to be weird, but here's my email address so we can talk more about bugs and trade articles about composting." Or "Making friends is hard, but

Alcohol and
SOCIALIZING

Booze is everywhere, and it's a fixture of socializing in many cultures. But when you are inviting new people to hang, don't assume that they drink alcohol. So many people don't drink at all or simply don't want to partake for a million different reasons. Unless you are positive they are enthusiastic about the idea, don't center your first hangout around drinking.

If you issue invitations to new friends that involve drinking, be sure to include booze-free options, too: "We could get coffee and dessert, or we could go to the museum's wine-and-mingle event. Which one sounds best to you?" Or "Coffee, tea, cocktails, or none of the above?"

If you're not drinking, you have every right to say, "Oh, I don't drink, so let's get tiramisu instead," or "I'm not into wine, but the museum still sounds great, let's do that." And if you're offered alcohol, you probably are already aware that you can say anything like, "No thanks, not tonight," or "Just water is fine," without providing further explanation. It's a reasonable decision, and, in turn, people should accept it without pressing.

I would like to give you my phone number so that you may text me memes. No pressure! See ya next week!"

LEAVE THE BALL IN THEIR COURT. Give *your* contact information first. That way, the other person can opt in. If Lauren from anime club can't meet on Tuesday, that is completely acceptable. Let her know that the offer still stands for the future, and if she's interested in hanging out another time, she can email you to get in touch. At that point, you've done all the correct things. If this friendship is meant to be, she will reach out through the designated channel. If she doesn't, let it go.

Dear Friendshipping,

When I meet new people, we have great conversations. But how do I know when it's the right time to reach out again?

Perhaps you'll find it comforting to know there is no exact right answer to this. Every situation is different. Individuals have different preferences. All we can do is try to be kind and welcoming without cornering or pressuring people. Here are some signs that it's probably a good moment to reach out:

1. **They gave you their contact info, and you've waited a little bit.** Let's say you met at the library's knitting circle that morning, and you exchanged social media handles. Go ahead and follow them. Then maybe wait a day or so before initiating a convo.

2. **You personally feel pretty good about it.** If you still feel weird about texting them after waiting for one day, wait another day. If you *still* feel hesitant after that, maybe you want to push yourself out of your comfort zone. Do you have evidence that is telling you not to reach out? Or is your internal anxiety getting to you? Either way, you need to feel at least pretty good about this to move forward.

3. **You actually have something to say.** If you can't think of a single thing to write, maybe wait a little longer. Your first text or email doesn't have to issue a formal invitation of friendship, though. It doesn't have to win a Pulitzer. It can be as simple as, "This hilarious internet post reminded me of our conversation," or "Here's the close-up picture of my philodendrons I promised you," or "Great meeting you at the dog park! Thanks for those extra poop bags, I'll bring some extra in case we run into each other next week."

MOVE ON, BUT DON'T GIVE UP. Not everyone is up for meeting people and making new friends at the exact same moment that you are interested in meeting people and making new friends. Some folks want to keep the relationship strictly in the classroom (or whatever setting you're in). That's totally allowed, and not necessarily a reflection on you as a person. Remember: eight billion people.

REMEMBER TO FOLLOW UP. If you do hang out, it was enjoyable, and you're noticing enthusiastic cues that they want to hang again, remember to follow up. You can initiate another invitation, too, but let this person weigh in on what the next hangout should look like. It's totally understandable to feel eager; just try to strike a relaxed, informal tone so you aren't pressuring them to put you on their calendar. (And you may do all of this well and still not get to hang out again anytime soon. People have busy lives, and it might be weeks and weeks before they can see you again.)

Don't forget to use your new tool: metathinking. When you start negative self-talk—*I'm bothering everyone when I speak up in these meetings; no one wants to hang out with me*—hit the pause button and ask yourself: *Wait, is that even true? Or am I just being incredibly hard on myself?* Making new friends—and keeping them—is a lifelong enterprise. Keep inviting people to hang out, keep offering hellos to new people, keep at it even when you feel discouraged; there is a long, joyous road unfolding at your feet. Maya Angelou said it best, as she so often did: "My wish for you is that you continue. Continue to be who and how you are, to astonish a mean world with your acts of kindness."

PART TWO

On Being Friends
The Common Issues

HOW TO HOST A GROUP HANGOUT

When you're inviting over friends you would like to get to know better, your first task is this: Imagine what the group would enjoy doing together. Is everyone drunk and playing Mario Kart? Or are they quietly bingeing episodes of *Mad Men*? Also consider *who* the guests would enjoy being around. Don't invite your entire volleyball team and then your coworker Molly who knows none of them. (Unless Molly is hella into volleyball and will therefore have a lot to talk about.) In other words, make a plan.

When you invite a crew somewhere without a planned activity, you are relying on your guests to entertain you and themselves. This worked in high school when everyone was hormonal and the very act

Dear Friendshipping,

My roommates and I have been getting more and more social and hosting movies and parties at our house. Recently we've been making more of an effort to invite one of my oldest friends over, but since then every movie turns into a conversation. I don't want to stop inviting her to events, but she doesn't seem to be able to sit through a movie without talking about several off-topic things. Do you have any ideas for how to dissuade conversation so we can enjoy movies again without excluding her?

Not everyone enjoys watching television shows and movies the same way. While you may require pin-drop silence as you absorb *Love & Basketball* for the ninetieth time, your friends might want to recite movie lines and provide commentary. So when your event revolves around watching something on a screen, you ought to get specific as to how you want this to go. You can include this info when you invite people to hang out. Consider one of the following options, in order of most to least concentration on watching:

- *Let's have a movie night. On Thursday, I'll put on* Love & Basketball. *A heated post-film discussion will take place over dessert.*

- *Let's watch* Love & Basketball *and recite every line we remember.*

- *Come to my place to drink too much wine while* Love & Basketball *plays in the background.*

In the moment when your friend is talking over the movie, it's OK to say, "I'll pause the movie if you want to talk." Or "In a few, let's take an intermission." Or, depending on your shared sense of humor, "This is my favorite part, don't make me throw a pillow at you."

of being in a room together outside of school was exciting. Sober adults need a little more guidance and stimulation. Some tactics from your teenage years still work, though: If you can't think of anything and you have a small budget, borrow a movie from the library. Did you know that many board games and card games have free files on the internet? You can download and print these games with just some paper. (Some of our faves: Root, Monikers, and Inhuman Conditions.)

When you know what you'd like to do and when, send an invitation with all the specifics. Setting extremely clear expectations, for any event, is a real courtesy. Plus, hosting is a lot of work, but the convenience of having your friends come to you is immense, so make it easy on them. Cover these topics in your invite:

THE WHEN: Old friends might already have an established pattern for hanging out. New friends do not. Give a time of arrival, and don't neglect to tell people when you want them to leave. ("Let's wrap up board games around midnight" and "get sloppy and crash on my floor" are both end-time options.) Let folks know if it's OK to roll in whenever, or if you're locking the doors and starting the movie at 8:00 p.m. sharp, with or without them.

THE WHERE: When you invite someone to your home for the first time, give a little more information than just your street address. Describe what your house or building looks like, how people can get in, where they can easily park—all the details. Look for any obstacles that you don't notice anymore (Is your buzzer working? Is your front door so heavy that people might mistake it as locked?) and keep accessibility in mind. Tell your friends if your place has lots of stairs or an elevator, or if you have a dog that jumps at new people (like Jenn's does). If it's a pain in the ass for others to get to or hang out at your home, change the location.

THE WHAT: Should people have dinner before showing up? Should they bring their favorite vinyl records? Explain the activity. Don't just say "Come over for a dinner party" and let your friends fill in the blanks.

Instead, try this: "I want to bake a lasagna, put on a new shirt, and have my adult friends over for dinner and conversation like they do on TV. Please bring a beverage other than wine, as I have that covered."

THE SIGNIFICANCE: If you're hosting an event that is especially important to you—a housewarming party in your new place after your divorce, a dinner where you are planning to cook an elaborate meal—make it abundantly clear that attendance really matters. You're not going to Hulk out if people can't attend; you're just saying, "Your attendance carries extra weight this time." This doesn't mean that everyone will be able to come, but they'll know to make room in their calendar if possible (and not to last-minute cancel if they can help it). However, you don't get to say this all the time. If you do, the meaning is lost. Not every event is OMG SO IMPORTANT. Explain your hopes for strong attendance in the invitation, like this: "I'm in charge of a fundraiser for work. I would love it if you could come by, even for ten minutes, because I really need people to fill the space." Or "This is Jessie's goodbye party before he moves to Alaska! I'm making individual savory pies ahead of time, so I need an accurate headcount and your preference of spinach, elk, or venison. Please let me know by Friday, thank you!" Or even simply: "I need ya to show up to this one, folks."

THE HOW: Extend the invitation through email, text, carrier pigeon, highway billboard, whatever feels right for the group. (Note: Don't put a bunch of people who don't know one another in the same group text.) For an event that requires lots of details and directions, we recommend using email so people can reference it easily. Remember that everyone has different habits for this kind of thing. Some people will RSVP in seconds, other people don't check their nonwork email every day. Some people will read texts, *think* they've answered them, but forget to actually respond. You may have to do individual follow-ups.

Here's an actual invitation that Trin once emailed to her friends. Feel free to plagiarize. (Just this invitation—not the entire book, please.)

Blaze-It Party
March 20, 6:30–9:30 p.m. (hard out)

Everyone come over on 3/20 to celebrate bisexual icon Fred Rogers's birthday! It will be the first day of spring, and I have baby plants to give away. Come by for any amount of time or even the entire time to have some Fun With Plants. It is acceptable to pop by, grab a plant, and leave! It's a Wednesday night, after all.

Activities:
• Plant discussions
• Plant eating (fruit salad)
• Plant vaping
• Plant watching (nature documentaries)

To bring:
• Plants, seeds, or cuttings (not required at all)
• Your partner! Just let me know if they're coming so I can have an updated head count and enough plants for all.

Getting here:
I live at 218 E Glass Street, 4B. You'll see my name on the buzzer at the gate. Take the elevator up to the fourth floor. My door will be the one with all the balloons on it.

I hope you can make it, but no worries if you cannot!

Please RSVP by responding to this email by Monday, March 18. Thank you!

Trin's invitation is a little much, just like her. But you don't need to plot out an itinerary for every gathering. Let your invite reflect your tone and personality. And when it's time to host, here are a few ways to make your place extra welcoming:

PLAN DRINKS AND SNACKS. Follow the two-hour rule. If your buds are hanging out for longer than two hours at your residence, you oughta offer snacks. The safest bet is plain potato chips. They're gluten-free and vegan (check the ingredients just in case). The only beverage you are required to provide is water, but make it clear to folks your party's BYOB. If you don't want alcohol at this event, say that in the invite, too. Ask about food allergies and restrictions ahead of time.

KEEP ACCESSIBILITY FRONT OF MIND. Be mindful of people who do not move through the world in the same way that you do. For example, plenty of folks can't stand for long periods of time. See about providing as much comfortable seating as your space can afford. Also, if you've got a pet, give everyone a heads-up in your invitation so people with concerns or allergies will know to bring meds or skip this particular event.

TELL PEOPLE WHAT TO BRING. If you plan to order pizza for everyone, let the group know if you want them to cover the costs of their dinner. There is nothing wrong with asking everyone to chip in (or bring a snack themselves), but it should be made clear when the invitation is given.

CLEAN YOUR BATHROOM. Take a moment to scrub down the counters, sinks, and most importantly, the toilet, which should not be a shade of brown. Stock your bathroom with toilet paper and hand soap. You aren't a convenience store, so it's not like you have to supply every possible toiletry, but if you can keep tampons, a plunger, and an air freshener visible in the bathroom, all the better.

HOW TO DEAL WITH CANCELLATIONS AND NO-SHOWS

When you plan any event, anticipate a smattering of last-minute cancellations. We can almost guarantee this will happen, and this doesn't reflect on you personally. People will get stuck at work, or decide they would rather have a quiet night at home, or need to take their dog to the vet. Traffic or weather could be unexpectedly uncooperative. The amount of effort needed to leave the house may simply be too much for your friend; choosing an outfit and tweezing every errant hair is often what it takes for many people to feel like they can present themselves to others.

These are all legitimate reasons to not attend—but still, we know it hurts if a friend backs out of plans at the last minute. As the host, you might expect (and deserve!) an explanation for why your friend cannot make your event. But you may simply not receive one. It takes vulnerability for a friend to say, "I got overwhelmed and going out tonight just felt like way too much," or "I have unholy farts right now that I'd rather not share with you." It's not like you're their boss or college professor; you don't require a note explaining their truancy. Give them the benefit of the doubt and assume they have a good, solid reason for not being there—no guilt trips allowed. Jenn's friend group established a blanket policy: Anyone can cancel plans at any time, no questions asked. If someone says they can't make it out after all, the others reply, "No problem, have a great night!" and truly mean it.

Work was pretty rough today. Could we move dinner to Tuesday?

No problem! Let's check in again tomorrow. Rest up!

Dear Friendshipping,

I had a bonfire at my place last weekend and invited my new cowork-ers. Four out of the six people ended up unable to go at the final hour. Is this a sign or something? Are we not really going to be friends?

Let's consider the fact that you invited coworkers. Coworkers are tricky! Maybe they misunderstood your invite and thought this was an optional networking event. Maybe they decided they see enough of one another during the work week. Did you invite a manager (or other kind of authority figure)? They might have felt like they couldn't cut loose with this person around. You also said that you are new to this job, so perhaps you misread how social and friendly your workplace is; it's time to step back and retake the social temperature of your office. And in the meantime, pursue a light and fun friendship with the people who did show up. Place your focus on the friendships that are working, not the ones that aren't.

Most of them are introverts who deeply understand one another's need to recharge alone, so they only make "soft" plans that do not involve pay-ing for tickets or making reservations ahead of time; i.e., "If you're up for it, let's meet for dinner on Friday. We can check in after work to see if we have the energy." In this way, they have given each other the gift of not feeling bad for canceling. It's a beautiful thing.

Sometimes plans just fail and it's nobody's fault. When Trin was in her twenties and worked at an awful desk job, she became friends with her coworkers who also hated their jobs. One friend attempted to throw a small get-together on a Friday night. Incidentally, that Friday afternoon everyone received their annual performance reviews. After reviews, every single person canceled on the party. No one felt like hang-ing out after receiving word that they were supposedly terrible at their jobs. The moral of this story: People will cancel for every kind of reason, and the reason probably has nothing to do with you. (And always check the work calendar when you make plans with coworkers.)

The absolute best way to get your friends to show up to your events: Have them infrequently. Yep! It's true. Especially for adults. If you're planning karaoke every Tuesday night for a group of thirty-five people and wondering why a month later people are bailing to catch up on TV, it's because they have event fatigue. Novelty gets people out the door.

Still, even the most novel plans can lead to the unfortunate phenomenon of bailing. Bailing is when someone says they will be there and then doesn't show up, without communicating—not even a text message. The first thing to do is make sure your friend is not having an emergency of some kind. Life is full of messes that need urgent attention. Find out if your friend is OK. Don't phone emergency services just yet, but send a simple message that requires only a short response: "Hey, we missed you at movie night. Just making sure everything is OK on your end," or "Just checking in! I didn't see you at movie night and want to make sure everything is A-OK." Assuming they respond—and they are indeed fine—you can certainly ask what happened. But first, do yourself a favor and consider the logistics of the event. Ask yourself:

DID YOUR FRIEND HAVE ALL THE INFORMATION? Ya gotta send that reminder text. "Hey, see you all tomorrow at 7:00 p.m. for movie night! Here's my address again." People are so terrible at remembering dates and times. The event may have been on *your* mind all day, but others' attention is elsewhere.

WAS EVERYONE ON THE SAME PAGE? If your guest's reply to your invitation included something along the lines of "I might make it" or "I'll try to pop by" or "I'll come over if I can," without any follow-up, they may have given you a Soft No.

WHEN WAS THE LAST TIME *YOU* BAILED? Perhaps your friend thinks this is all totally normal—that this is simply part of your dynamic, and that telling you they won't be there is an unnecessary formality. You both may have established a pattern of bailing without even realizing it.

If your friend's absence still doesn't make sense after answering those questions, you certainly can ask your friend why they didn't show up. We recommend doing this a day or two after the event so you're able to clearly articulate yourself and how you feel. Your friend may have forgotten completely; they may have prioritized something else over you; they may have thought your event wasn't a big deal and that you wouldn't even notice their absence. Maybe your friend is going through something stressful and their attention is totally frayed, or perhaps it was just a simple miscommunication. Life is full of mistakes and blunders and social errors. Bottom line: You can be an understanding and kind person, and at the same time, you can hold your friends to what they say. You deserve friends who are reliable, enjoy your company, and show up when they say they will. It is worth asking what happened, but you don't have to like the answer you get.

THE HIGHS AND LOWS OF CANCELING PLANS

HOW TO COPE WITH FLAKY FRIENDS

Canceling plans can be an enormous relief. Adults usually have no time or energy to spare, and even the most extroverted and social person will occasionally want to allocate their waking hours differently from how they had previously scheduled them. Of course, it does hurt to be canceled upon over and over again, especially if you established plans and/or spent money far in advance.

Dear Friendshipping,

When I invite my friends over, there are three common reactions: no response at all, a thumbs-up emoji that I interpret as a yes but then they don't show, and an outright yes that becomes a no minutes before the activity. How do I get my friends to be clear about when they can hang out?

Good friends don't want to hurt you. But some friends don't know that the thing they are doing hurts. It sounds like this pattern has established itself in your friend group, so let's break the pattern. First, take a break from inviting your friends over. You could probably use some time off from hosting duties (and there's a chance that your buds are just fatigued of one another; this happens), and most of this problem will solve itself. Then, in a few weeks, issue a brand new invitation, and issue it differently than you have in the past. Use different language; make it a more established, "important" event; basically, make it more than just a casual hangout. If your friends haven't responded enthusiastically to watching TV together at your place, change the activity or the venue. And don't forget to use your words to say specifically what you need: "Hi all. Let me know by tonight if you are a 'yes, will definitely be there' for tomorrow's brunch."

Let's say your friend RSVPs yes to your event but then, for the fourth time in a row, they cancel at the last minute. If your friend has a pattern of canceling like this and it's starting to hurt your feelings, it's worth bringing it up to them and having a serious discussion. But first, consider what you want to get out of it. How do you hope your friend will answer? With a decent explanation? A sincere apology? There are dozens of ways you can bring this up, so consider how you'll do it and how you *think* they'll respond. Basically, brainstorm the convo first so you feel prepared. The goal: to be able to look back on the conversation without regret, knowing that you handled it well. Here are some ways to start (insert the specifics of your situation):

- *This is the fourth time you've canceled at the last minute. I wanted to see if you are doing all right. Would it be easier for you if I counted you as "tentative" in the future?* It's certainly a possibility that something bigger is going on with your friend, and it's a kindness to give them the opportunity to say so.
- *Hey, I [put my own stuff on hold / cleaned my apartment / baked your favorite pie from scratch] because I expected you to be here. I don't want you to feel terrible, but I do want you to make it up to me by [setting up a new coffee date / cleaning your own apartment / baking me a pie from scratch]. Deal?* Using both humor and honesty might just make the whole conversation easier on both of you. Plus, you are telling your friend exactly how to make it up to you.
- *I was really looking forward to seeing you.* Maybe you just want your friend to know that their actions have an impact on your feelings. Be honest without pressuring them— simply explain how their absence made you feel.
- *This is happening enough these days that it's starting to bum me out. Is there something I can do to help you make it to stuff I plan? Would it be less stressful for you if I invited you out less?* You're a) letting them know their actions matter to you, and b) making a plan to prevent this from happening again. If you make an offer like this, you have to hold up your end of the deal.

Do not:

CONTINUE TO INVITE PEOPLE WHO NEVER SHOW UP. You deserve friends who honor their commitments and make time for you.

PRESSURE PEOPLE. Don't insist that someone come over, have one more drink, play one more round, or stay for one more hour.

DEMAND AN EXPLANATION. You can ask what's up with your friend, but don't start a debate about the when, where, and why. You are not a parent demanding to know why their kid missed curfew.

But do:

PLAN FEWER EVENTS. Make the ones you do plan super special so people know that they're important.

BEFRIEND PEOPLE WHO WANT TO SPEND THEIR TIME THE SAME WAY YOU DO. Everyone has a well of social energy. Some people have a deep well. For others, it's quite shallow. If you get your kicks by going out often, but you've mistakenly befriended only introverts who live in caves, it's time to branch out. You may need some folks in your life who get energized by lots of company, not drained by it.

CONSIDER ONLINE HANGOUTS. The internet is a mixed bag in terms of how it has affected human relationships. One *actual* good thing that has come out of it is The Online Hangout. Watching a movie or playing tabletop RPGs with your friends over Skype is a great way to find a middle ground with your introverted friends and cut out the time suck of cleaning your place and grooming yourself.

THROW THINGS TOGETHER AT THE LAST MINUTE. This sounds counterintuitive, we know, but if you get together at the absolute second you feel like doing something, your friends won't have time to cancel, talk themselves out of attending, or make other plans. If it's 7:00 p.m. on Saturday and you want to eat a pizza at 7:30 p.m., text all your friends *right there and then* to see who can join in. You might be surprised by the response.

GUILTY AS CHARGED: WHEN YOU'RE THE ONE WHO ALWAYS CANCELS

It's completely acceptable to cancel plans when you need to. You are not a monster. But if you are a serial canceler, you are probably starting to bum out your friends, and eventually they may stop inviting you to stuff. We don't want you to undervalue your presence in your friends' lives. It's meaningful when you show up and you are missed when you don't—your friends love you and they want to see you. While it's healthy and practical to take the pressure off of canceling plans, remember that some events are simply better with you there.

If you want to change your habit of canceling, try being way, way more honest with yourself about what you like to do and when you like to do it. Everyone optimistically says *hell yes* to hanging out on Friday

Dear Friendshipping,

I have a lot on my plate right now, so I have had to cancel last-minute on a few friend hangouts. It's making me nervous that my friends will get sick of this and of me. Is it bad to cancel plans all the time?

If you are consistently canceling plans, you are making too many plans. Sounds like it's time for you to streamline your life. Figure out the short-term stuff that you *need* to do (finish that overdue essay, get to work on time, create some downtime for yourself), and then what you would *like* to do (see friends). It's OK to put your head down and take care of yourself and your immediate to-do list. We don't want you to completely neglect your friendships, because companionship is good for you, but you can shift your priorities for the moment. In the meantime, text your friends, send emails, check in when you want/can; socialize from afar. Adults know what it's like to be overwhelmed—we bet your friends will understand!

night when they're in a good mood on Friday morning. But sometimes that good mood can be untrustworthy. If you work a 9-to-5 type of job, Friday becomes the most flakeable day of the week. Use the fantastic power of your imagination to visualize how you will feel when you return home after a long day. Are you really going to want to leave your house again? Don't lie to us now.

When you're invited out, you don't need to immediately respond with "Yes, I'll be there!" to be nice and polite. You can decline both politely and truthfully! Expand your vocabulary. Here are some examples of respectful declines and less committed responses:

- *Thank you for thinking of me. Can I let you know the day of if I can make it?*
- *This sounds awesome. Right now my attendance is dependent on [my teething baby / our unreliable puppy-sitter / final exams / my travel schedule], so I can't say yes just yet.*
- *I would love to go, but for the foreseeable future, my schedule is dedicated to [getting over this cold / packing up my house to move / spending time with my grandmother / grading a ton of papers], so I can't commit to this right now. I really appreciate you taking the time to invite me.*
- *Thanks for inviting me out! I'll get back to you with an answer tomorrow, if that's OK. I'm going to see if that works with my schedule.*
- *I'm a tentative yes at this point, but I won't know for sure until the morning of. Is that OK? If not, I'll say no now.*
- *I'm sorry, I'm not going to be able to make this one. I really appreciate how patient you are when I am so busy!*

This way, you're either setting expectations clearly (your attendance is not guaranteed), or you're turning down the invitation before you can cancel. It's kinder to decline initially than to cancel at the last minute. Or, you can delay your decision until you are in the right frame of mind to be honest with yourself. You're removing the pressure to decide your future attendance in the present moment.

All that said, if you picked up this book because you are dissatisfied with how many friends you have or with the level of intimacy you have with your current friends, maybe it's time to change things up. The company of kind people who love you is a necessary ingredient for a healthy life. Good friends lighten your burdens. Replenish your energy. Make you hate yourself a little less. So maybe you need to review your schedule and allocate more time for seeing your friends or consider expanding your social parameters. Maybe go out more instead of staying in. And we don't mean just to loud bars and parties—if that's not your idea of fun, it doesn't ever need to be. But wherever you're going, sometimes you need a little kick in the ass to get yourself motivated. Here are some tricks that might help you out:

- Chug a glass of ice water or drink some caffeine, if that's your thing.
- Go straight to the event after work or school. Don't stop at home.
- If you do stop at home, do not lie down on your couch or bed. Don't even look at your bed! You know what'll happen if you do. You'll just go to sleep or watch British reality television all night. (If this is something you're doing consistently, it's worth figuring out why. Are you getting enough sleep?)

- Put on clothing that makes you feel good and that you wouldn't lounge in at home by yourself—not only will wearing your sequined pants make you feel more upbeat, they are uncomfortable to sleep in.
- Put on loud dancy music. Sing in the shower. Keep your energy up in whatever way feels best for you.

When we spend enough time away from activities, we occasionally build up what is annoying about them (getting out of your pajamas, commuting, bad weather, exhaustion) and not what is *enjoyable* about them. Remind yourself of the fun parts, recall the great nights you've had out, and assess if it's worth the effort to get out the door. It really might be!

Also consider where you go and what you do with your friends. What settings drain you of energy? Alternatively, what settings do you thrive in? Jenn's fave thing to do with friends: long, loud restaurant dinners with lots of courses of food and wine and lively conversation. Sounds fun, right?! Well, not everyone cares about restaurant cuisine or wants to pay for it (totally understandable), and not everyone drinks alcohol (also totally understandable). It would be silly to always accept this invitation if it's not your thing. If you haven't yet found your thing, try an activity that doesn't require a lot of your social energy, like seeing a movie or a play. You can enjoy companionship in this setting but you also have room to relax and not hold an extended conversation. Board games help with this, too. Playing a game with a group does require your attention, but it also acts as a social buffer.

But if none of this rings true with you—it's not your level of energy or the event itself that is making you cancel constantly—it's gotta be something else. Examine your habits. It could be:

YOU ACCEPT EVERY INVITE. Do you feel obligated to say yes to every single invitation thrown your way? Or is someone pressuring you to come out all the time? Because that is not how you deserve to be treated. You are allowed to turn down invitations, and good friends will prioritize your comfort over their need to throw a bangin' barbeque. Take a beat before accepting the next invitation and consider whether you truly want to go.

YOU'RE OVERBOOKING YOURSELF ON PURPOSE. Some people, including the authors of this book, overschedule themselves so they don't have any extra time to think, breathe, or worry. Instead of filling your schedule with too many fun events (that you may or may not cancel), distract yourself from your problems with a craft, video game, or other solo activity that you can pick up and put down whenever you need some sweet, soothing denial.

IN YOUR HEART OF HEARTS, YOU DON'T ACTUALLY LIKE YOUR FRIEND(S). If you experience consistent feelings of dread before spending time with someone, that's probably a sign that they're not right for you. This is an important realization to have in adulthood (more on this later).

And if it's still none of these things, you may just need a break from in-person hangouts for a while. Put up a metaphorical "do not disturb" sign while you get more sleep and align your priorities. We do not advocate completely distancing yourself from your friends or suddenly ignoring their messages—we are just telling you that it's wise to take social breaks if that's

what you need. Give your friend(s) a heads-up, too. If you were going out of town for six weeks, you would let people know, right? Think of this as taking a mental and social vacation. You don't need to get into the details (unless you feel like it), but here are a few ideas:

- *Hi everybody, I'm going to be unavailable for a bit because I'm taking a social break. I'll poke my head out again after the holidays!*
- *Thanks so much for thinking of me. I'm sorry that I can't make it that night. I'm feeling burnt out and need to stay in. Give me a few weeks to recharge and then let's do something fun.*
- *Hello, my dear! Just wanted to let you know I'm busy [finding a new apartment / studying for finals / managing a big project at work / traveling with my family] these days, so I'll be taking lunch alone to cool down from all of that.*
- *If I disappear from the group chat, I'm all good! Just focusing on other things right now.*
- *Hi all, wanted to let you know that I'm out for our Wednesday trivia night for the next few weeks. I'm still planning to come to our movie night next month! See you then!*

Don't forget that you can socialize without leaving your home. The pandemic taught us all about seeing friends from a distance, remember? Text a friend while you watch the same movie, use group video chat to play Pictionary, demand to see pets over FaceTime. You can do all of this in your pajamas! It's totally possible to hang with your friends while protecting your limited well of energy.

FRIENDS AND SOCIAL MEDIA

HEY, JEALOUSY: ON SOCIAL MEDIA ENVY

When you see photos online of your friends having fun, and those photos make you experience feelings of doubt or insignificance, first acknowledge exactly what is happening in your head and heart. Name the emotion. (Hint: It's jealousy!) Don't disguise the feeling, pretend that jealousy is beneath you, or make it seem scarier than it is. Recognize that you are feeling envy—which is normal—and then examine it more closely with metathinking:

> - *OK, so I'm feeling jealous. Why? Is it because I wish I had been invited, too? Is this a reasonable request or an unreasonable request?*
> - *Is this actually a dig against me, or am I just being unfair to myself?*
> - *I feel left out. If I want to see my friend more often, should I initiate plans myself?*
> - *Does my friend having fun with other people hurt or impact me at all? If I want the best for my friend, that means letting them have a rich social life.*
> - *Of course I want my friends to have fun in life. What would the opposite be—only hanging out with one person forever?*
> - *Is this a problem I need to work on, or is this just a passing feeling I'll get over in a moment?*

A little envy is simply a sign that you care. It only becomes a problem if the feeling swells into a tidal wave or causes you to treat people unfairly, like making rules or demands. Even envy that is rooted in goodness—*I love my friend, I miss their company, I only want to hang*

out more!—does not entitle anyone to anyone else's time or attention. Feelings of hurt do not justify this kind of encroaching, controlling behavior.

And remember, the platforms themselves play a tremendous part in sparking these feelings within you. Social media is life's highlight reel. We use it to share our lives and connect with people, but it's also a kind of performance art. We post our wittiest observations, our most vibrant sunset pics, our hottest takes, and our carefully selected selfies. It's editing. Curating. Of course you are not your entire self online—you present a version of yourself. There's nothing wrong with this, either! Do you behave the same way around your boss as you do your sister? Hell no. Each day, you amplify and exaggerate, curtail and downplay. You have a personal filter. It's the same online. You are only getting a small peek into someone's life, and jealousy is filling in the blanks: *They're having so much fun without me!*

If social media is feeding your jealousy, it's time to use it much differently (or much less). Here are some ideas on de-escalating social media in your life:

How to Keep It #Blessed
ON SOCIAL MEDIA

Everyone uses social media differently. What seems routine to you is not routine to all your friends. While you're microblogging about gourmet cheeseburgers, another friend is posting sexy selfies, while a different pal is on Twitter solely to complain to Delta customer service. All valid!

Some people use social media more or less frequently than you. Maybe you check Twitter every forty seconds, while some of your friends might only glance at their feed during their commute or over the weekend. Regardless of how much you use social media, here's what to keep in mind:

- You are not obligated to "like" or "fave" or respond to every single thing your friends post, and it's usually considered creepy to interact with posts—especially photos—that are months and months old. (Save those likes for your close friends, not that coworker you grabbed coffee with once.)

- No one can hear your tone, and all comments are open to misinterpretations. For example, something like, "Excuse me, how come we haven't hung out in forever?!" might read as passive aggressive rather than excited or friendly.

- If your friend uses social media primarily for professional purposes, act accordingly. Maybe they're a teacher with an audience of students, a real estate agent interacting with clients, or a freelance illustrator seeking commissions. Avoid leaving your hilarious-but-dirty inside jokes on public or client-facing posts.

- Speaking of business: If it helps your friends to share, review, repost, retweet, or reblog their work and projects, consider doing it! It's a nice friendship move and an easy way to show support.

- Get offline and reach out to a friend you haven't seen or spoken to recently (make sure it's one who will be delighted to hear from you).
- Fill your feed with happy stuff, like just-adopted rescue pets.
- Give your brain a break and institute time limits. For example, no Instagram after 9:00 p.m., or only thirty minutes of scrolling per day.
- Turn off all notifications.
- Leave your phone in a different room and watch a movie. (Then congratulate yourself for being the first person in history to successfully do this.)
- Start following interesting people who have nothing to do with your social life, like chefs or cartoonists or urban farmers. The entire breadth of the internet is at your fingertips, and you can use it to do more than watch from afar as your friends drink wine spritzers.
- Throw your phone in a lake.

If these ideas don't work for you, you may need to do the unthinkable: Unfollow your friends or mute their feeds. Yes, really. What can you control in this situation? Not what your friends post to social media, that's for sure— they can do whatever they like. But you  *can* control your own habits. You have the power to feel more joy and less jealousy. In fact, if social media is impacting how you treat people, we would argue it is your *responsibility* to change how you use it. Consider the worst-case scenario here: When you're absorbing negative feelings

Dear Friendshipping,

I travel a lot for my job, and I'm gone for weeks at a time. That means I am often privy to my friends' lives only over social media. I always feel a little sad when I see photos of them all hanging out while I'm alone in a hotel. To be clear, I love my job, and I love traveling. This is really the only downside to it. Do you have any ideas on how to navigate these weird feelings?

Make plans to look forward to. Get on your friends' calendars. And in the meantime, if it makes you sad to look at their social media while you're on the road, mute them for now. You can even unmute them and catch up on all of their posts right before you see them in person. Another note: Kicking ass at your job is wonderful. Spending time with people who love you is also wonderful and a vital part of your health as a person. If your job gets in the way of your ability to do that, consider that you might be hustling too hard! But we get it. Sometimes it truly is worth making sacrifices, like spending less time with your friends. If it's within your control, try to make missing your friends a short-term sacrifice instead of a long-term one.

over and over, these feelings could build and build until you feel genuine resentment. Or maybe you'll just become impatient and irritable. By limiting your social media intake, you are making a grown-up decision. As an adult, you are responsible for discovering what kinds of situations will make you act poorly. Then you must either a) not act poorly, or b) remove yourself from the situation.

Taking a break from social media doesn't have to mean you are taking a break from friendship entirely. You're just taking a hiatus from something that is making you unhappy. And besides, you, too, have a highlight reel. We know that sounds silly, but it's true. It just might not be on social media. Flip through a pile of photos. Reread old text messages from friends. Social media is tricking you into thinking you have less than you need. Take a moment to take stock of what you already have.

WHY IT'S TOTALLY OK TO UNFOLLOW YOUR FRIENDS

Disengaging with friends on social media is such a modern problem that there really aren't well-known rules of etiquette. Let's write some now, starting with this: Your friends are allowed to unfollow or mute you on any social media platform, at any time. You, too, are allowed to unfollow or mute anyone on any social media platform, at any time. This is not a signal that your friendship is over, or that you now hate each other, or that it's time to fight this out. No one would ever sign a contract that states "Friends must never look away from each other's social media posts, photography, selfies, vacation photos, personal poetry, political manifestos, and hot takes. They must enjoy each other's presence both online and offline, 24/7, without a single pause." Such a contract would be completely untenable. No friendship would survive it.

We can control so, so little of what we see each day online. Curating who you follow is a rare opportunity to choose what messages enter your atmosphere. You're a grown-up with preferences and opinions. You oughta listen to them. You are not going to police your friend's behavior on Twitter or tell them to quiet down with the politics or post fewer selfies. You are simply doing the equivalent of taking a step into another room for a few minutes for your own well-being. That's so understandable. And to be clear, we don't advocate completely averting your attention and ignoring what is unfolding in the world, in your community, or in the lives of your friends. We *do* advocate

protecting your mental health and patience level. If you are removing yourself from a situation in which you feel anxiety, resentment, or annoyance, you are making a mature decision so that you can remain a kind friend.

By the way, you can do more than mute and unfollow if you need to. If this person is spewing hateful garbage online, the problem is not just their internet etiquette. (More on this on page 195.)

Finally Hitting That Unfollow Button

If you unfollow someone, they may notice, get upset, and ask you about it; they may take this personally. And look, we get why: It feels like a slight, even if it's not intended as such. People often default to the worst-case scenario when they are feeling hurt. They may interpret the unfollowing as you saying "Don't talk to me!" or "I never liked you that much." So if/when you unfollow your friend, we want you to be prepared for them to be a little (or a lot) upset. You can provide a white lie or a reason for your actions, but you don't have to. If they flat-out ask you why you unfollowed them, here are some scripts:

- *I try to keep my social media feed pretty light so I don't miss updates from [my family / politics / the field I work in].*
- *I'm just not into the stuff you're into, and I'm culling the list of people I follow.*
- *I tend to use social media more for networking and less for having conversations with friends.*
- *I'm unfollowing a lot of people and taking a break.*
- *I decided that as much as I love X-rated fan art, it's not what I want popping up on my phone.*

What It Means (and Doesn't Mean) When You're Unfollowed

If you are the one who is unfollowed, and you are feeling hurt and confused, take a moment to consider all the benign possibilities at play here. Maybe your friend:

HAS PRIVACY CONCERNS. It could be that they're quietly locking down their account because they want to start posting personal info and can't chance having it leak. This could be a matter of risk or safety.

WANTS TO SPEND LESS TIME ONLINE OR ON THEIR PHONE. Good for them. Social media can be distracting, toxic, and a real bummer. The fewer people there, the less tempting it is to refresh and refresh and refresh until your eyes fall out.

IS NOT THAT INTERESTED IN WHAT YOU'RE TALKING ABOUT. You don't need your friends to share your every single hobby, right? If your friend doesn't enjoy the outdoors, you wouldn't expect them to join your weekly hike. Same idea here. If you like to post daily missives about philosophers and your pal unfollows you, they probably just aren't that interested in Descartes. No big deal.

WANTS TO KEEP IT KID-FRIENDLY OR STRICTLY PROFESSIONAL. If your friend is looking to network, find new jobs, or promote their work, they might unfriend anyone who isn't keeping it profesh, too. This isn't a judgment call on you—they aren't asking you to change anything about what you share or write or post. *You* keep on sharing that naughty fanfiction, you little vixen, you.

MADE A MISTAKE. It's easy to accidentally hit unfriend/unfollow. We've both done it!

Please remind yourself—repeatedly, if necessary—that when a friend unfollows or mutes you online, they are not breaking any friendship laws. They're allowed to unfollow anyone they wish, as are you! Your friend is not punishing you or being mean. They are simply saying to themselves, "Eh, I don't want to read this right now, thanks." Isn't that understandable? We hope you will take this to heart, and that you won't reach out to the person and ask, "Hey, why did you unfollow me? What gives?" This question does not open doors for productive conversation because:

- It's inappropriate to sidestep someone's clear request not to interact with you.
- You are putting a friend in an awkward and defensive position.
- Unfollowing a person on social media isn't a rejection of them wholesale.
- You'll probably get more upset. If they gave you an honest reason why, would you change your behavior? Or would you just become angrier?
- It's *just* social media. C'mon. There are cute pet parakeets with ten thousand more Instagram followers than you.

If you truly believe that you can have a mature and productive conversation about this, fine, go ahead, but don't flood their inbox demanding to know what happened. That's definitely an invasion of their space and a waste of your energy. Give it time. Change your habits. You may be surprised by what switching things up can do for you.

THE CARE AND KEEPING OF
LONG-DISTANCE FRIENDSHIPS

When long distance enters a friendship, your relationship will evolve and change. Fortunately, this does not signal the end of the friendship; it just signals a *new kind* of friendship. Our first piece of advice: Find the absolute easiest, least complicated way for you to talk—one that works for both parties. Before the move happens, you may be tempted to establish strict keep-in-touch plans that you have not tested out: "We will play co-op computer games and shout at each other online every weekend." Or "Email every single time you go on a date with someone new and spare no details." Or "We shall gab on the phone every Sunday night for forty-five minutes for our mandatory friendship time." We understand why you'd want to make plans ahead of time—you want reassurance that you'll stay close. But your plans might not pan out so well in reality. If you miss a phone call or email, you'll feel guilty. Or what if you're just not in the mood to chat when Sunday night rolls around? Make it as easy as you possibly can on yourself and your friend to connect. Catch up in a way that is low-stress, allows for flexibility, and doesn't come with obligations.

And when you do connect with each other, recognize how awesome that is. Now that you are long distance, the little things—emails, comments on your social media, the short and sweet text messages—matter more. When your friend takes time from their busy and faraway life to reach out to you, that should mean a little more than any ol' text message. You're on their mind! How nice. And when they cross *your* mind, tell them so.

Your friendship can survive a change of scenery, but prepare for an adjustment period as you find your sea legs. Here are some other ideas for staying close with a long-distance friend:

EXAMINE YOUR OWN COMMUNICATION HABITS. If you don't regularly ask questions like "What's new with you? / How are you? / How was your day?" now is the perfect time to add these friendly phrases to your vocab. If you tend to ignore your phone (don't blame you) or rarely answer text messages, change it up. If you're not much of a sharer, it's time to get in the habit of talking about your life. You may not be well practiced with sharing because your friend is usually there to live it with you. That's not true anymore. Give updates. Send photos. Talk about how your spouse is doing, the furniture you are painting, the new brewery you toured, the job you are going to apply for. It doesn't have to be over a phone call—don't strain yourself to use the phone if you never do—but you can safely assume your friend cares about what is happening in your life.

BE PREPARED FOR SOME FOMO. That means *fear of missing out*. When you see glimpses of your long-distance friend's life on social media,

Dear Friendshipping,

I just moved to a new city. I'm nervous about making friends, but I'm more nervous about missing the friends I have. We have already made plans and they bought plane tickets to come visit me. But when I see pictures of their hangouts on social media, I feel so sad and jealous! How do I handle this?

One day, you will be able to look at your friends' photos and not feel sadness. But today is not that day! You're not there yet. You are processing a major change in your life. And while you're processing, it's OK to mute your friends' feeds. They never have to know about it. It can be like a secret gift you can give yourself. Or you can tell them about it: "Hey friends, just wanted to let you know that moving sucks so much that I need to mute you on social media until I can stop being jealous that you all still get to hang out and I don't. If you make any major announcements on Facebook while I'm on a break, I'll miss them, so keep me in the loop in another way!"

surrounded by people you've never met and looking like they are having the time of their life, your first reaction might be sadness and jealousy. Now you're finding out that they are starring in the local production of *Peter Pan* through a Facebook status update?! How dare they not call you! A little jealousy is normal, but you need to chill out and not act on it. Your friend doesn't need to hit pause on their life just because you are not there.

UNDERSTAND THAT YOUR FRIEND WILL MAKE NEW FRIENDS. At some point you may notice that your friend is somehow doing fine without you nearby. Maybe that makes you feel relieved and delighted on their behalf, or maybe it makes you feel a little sad, like you're on the sidelines instead of in the game with them. But the sidelines are very important—that's where your teammates rest between crucial plays!

Cheering you on! You're still a crucial member of the team even if you're on the bench.

TENDING TO YOUR CACTUS FRIENDS

But what if your friend just isn't easy to get ahold of? What if you can't seem to connect with any regularity? That isn't a sign that the friendship is failing or that you are not important anymore. Maybe they are the type of person who simply doesn't need consistent communication to maintain a friendship. Our friend Kate coined the term "cactus friend," and we love it so much we decided to borrow it: Cactus friends are people who do not require a lot of sunlight and watering (or conversation and visits). Do you have a cactus friend on your hands? What about you, though—are you an orchid? Orchids need more care. There's nothing wrong with either plant. You simply require different amounts of water and attention to grow and feel nurtured. OK, this metaphor is getting ridiculous. Basically: You and your friend may have mismatched communication styles, but that does not mean you are incompatible. It just means the two of you need to be flexible and honest with each other about what you need.

VISITING YOUR LONG-DISTANCE FRIENDS

Visiting your friend isn't necessary to keep up the friendship, but if you have the money and time to spare, plan a trip to go see 'em. Here are a few things to keep in mind when you visit a long-distance pal, because things will be a little different (or very different) from the last time you saw them in person:

DON'T ASSUME THAT YOU CAN CRASH ON YOUR FRIEND'S FLOOR FOR FIVE NIGHTS, EVEN IF YOU ARE THE BEST OF FRIENDS. Don't assume that you can crash for even *one* night. You have to use your words and ask out loud if this is an option and then be prepared for any kind of answer. There are plenty of well-founded reasons why staying at their place may not work out—unhappy roommates, lack of physical space, difficult pets, busy schedules, or anxiety about having people in their house for days at a time.

YOUR FRIEND IS HOSTING YOU, SO YOU SHOULD DISCUSS BEFORE-HAND WHAT THAT MEANS. Are they going to take time off from work to hang out with you each day? Are they going to be out the door at 8:00 a.m., but plan to meet you for dinner each night that you're in town? Is there an itinerary, or is it a casual, make-no-plans kind of trip? Are you comfortable doing things on your own? If so, how are you going to get around? If they have a car, are you going to borrow it? (If so, you oughta return it with the gas tank full, by the way.)

BE A FANTASTIC AND COURTEOUS HOUSEGUEST. You will never have a full account of what kind of roommate or houseguest you are because you only have your own perspective. But at the very least you should be able to say to yourself with confidence, "I know for sure that I am a polite guest because I do my dishes instead of leaving them in the living room, always flush the toilet, replace the toilet paper roll when it's done, apologize and/or replace things if I break them, say please and thank you, don't leave messes for other people to clean up, offer to walk the dog / pick up a bottle of wine / make breakfast / do some kind of chore, and understand that the host will not be available to me 24/7."

Change is hard, but friendships can survive long distance. Some can even quietly *thrive* on long distance. A friend's absence might make you appreciate them more than ever before; visiting could be the high-light of your whole year; and, hey, sometimes it just feels nice to be missed.

For twelve years, Jenn lived time zones away from her best childhood friend Nadija. In those days, they used just about every method of keeping in touch available: AIM chat rooms! Postcards! Phone calls on an actual telephone! Despite their hard work, life still occasionally got in the way. Jenn turned into such a cactus friend that at times the two went months without talking. But their relationship shifted to fit the circumstances, and Nadija learned to accept Jenn's new watering schedule. Their dedication prevailed, and these days they're finally living in the same city. They were even the maid-of-honor in each other's weddings. If there's one thing we know for sure, it's that distance doesn't have to be an ending of any kind.

THE SHARING AND KEEPING OF SECRETS

SPILLING YOUR SECRETS

Secrets are like little gifts to give and receive from your friends. As you get closer to a person, you give them more and more of these little gifts, like the gritty details of your divorce, how you really feel about your roommates, or who you've been banging. Typically, the dearer a person is to you, the more of your gifts that person will come to possess. Secrets bring you closer to fully understanding each other. It's a risk every single time you share a secret, but that risk could be worth taking, since the exchanging of personal info is how people bond. Imagine if you never shared a single embarrassing or intimate anecdote about yourself—that's a difficult path to making friends and letting people get to know you. Still, when you share your private info, remember:

BE CLEAR AND SPECIFIC ABOUT WHAT YOU'RE DISCLOSING. State what is *actually* private and what is shareable. This distinction is something you must define very clearly, out loud, and probably more than once. Humans do not have universally agreed upon rules for this, so you have to make 'em yourself. For example, you may have just assumed that your best friend would carry the secret of your bed-wetting to their grave. But maybe they understand that bed-wetting can come from a combination of environmental, genetic, and physiological problems that were not your fault, and therefore didn't think it was that big of a deal when they mentioned it offhand to their entire family. Begin the conversation with your request for privacy, like this:

- *I want to tell you about this horrific first date, but can you promise me that you won't tell anyone?*
- *I have a story for you, but I need ya to keep this between us.*
- *Want to hear about the worst job interview I ever had? You can tell other people about it, just don't share the name of the company, please and thank you.*

YOU'RE CREATING A DIVISION (THIS APPLIES ESPECIALLY TO GROUPS OF FRIENDS). Once you tell your secret to a few people, you have drawn an invisible line between who knows and who doesn't. That might be perfectly OK with you, or maybe you decide it's too much of a risk. The fewer people who know, the safer you are! Historically, rebellions have succeeded when information is kept on a need-to-know basis so that nothing leaks to the enemy in the event of a capture.

FRIENDS TELL THEIR LOVED ONES STUFF. For better or worse, your friends—even your closest friends—will probably think it's OK to share your secrets with their partners / spouses / boyfriends / girlfriends. Some people tell their mom everything. Others will immediately text secrets to all their siblings. People do this because it feels like telling only their innermost circle is the same as keeping the secret to themselves. You can certainly request that they don't do this, but you must say that specifically: "I know this is a big ask, but I want to keep this one only between us! Not even your mother! Deal?" Or "I have to tell you something about your husband's coworker, but first, can you promise you won't share it with your husband?"

KEEPING YOUR FRIENDS' SECRETS

You are responsible for keeping secrets when your friends ask. Secret keeping demonstrates your integrity and accountability. You want to be someone your friends can trust! (Of course, there will always be exceptions to these rules: Some promises must be broken; some secrets need to be shared—we're referring to matters of safety and danger.) But for the secrets that are important but not dire, here are some tips on how to keep them (because we know it can be difficult to do!):

OPTING OUT IS ALWAYS AN OPTION. Know the risks: What if you get tipsy and spill the secret? What if your mom / best friend / partner finds out that you knew this secret the whole damn time and you didn't tell her and now she's pissed as hell? If someone asks you to keep a secret and you just don't want that kind of responsibility and pressure (understandable), you can say, "Please don't tell me anything I can't share." Or "Before you say anything, please don't tell me anything I can't also tell Nadija, because I tell Nadija basically everything." This is the mature thing to do. You don't have to know everything to be someone's friend, and it's impossible to unknow a piece of vital information.

BE HONEST ABOUT YOUR SECRET-KEEPING ABILITIES. Do you often feel tempted to share? Are you just bad at keeping secrets? Lots of people are, and it's mature and responsible to acknowledge this about yourself and accept that secrets are not your strength. When someone is about to give you an especially juicy and interesting secret, they're basically saying, "Here's $400. You can never, ever spend it." You know better than to pocket that money!

REMEMBER THAT BLABBERMOUTHS GET FOUND OUT. And they get reputations. Repeatedly sharing other people's private info often comes from a place of insecurity. If you're desperately craving a bond with someone, it's easy to resort to gossiping to get that fix. But you are responsible for controlling the impulse. Once you share a secret, you can't control what happens next. The secret takes on a life of its own. So if you're holding in a secret so juicy that you have to tell someone or you'll explode, tell your dog, your fish, or your trustworthy aunt who lives abroad and has zero connections to the people involved.

Dear Friendshipping,

I aired some dirty laundry to a friend, only to find out that she shared it with her roommates. My friend was actually shocked that I was upset. She apologized, but she also said that she had no idea what I told her was confidential. I shared intensely personal stuff about my love life, some family history, and so on, so that seems hard to believe. How can I prevent this from ever happening again?

Everyone has a different definition of what information is personal and when that information can be shared. Your friend clearly has a very different definition of what is public-facing information. When you're both feeling clear-headed, consider talking it out. Lay out what you need to change in the future. "Don't ever talk about me to another person" is an unrealistic guideline, but "Please don't tell anyone about who I smooch" is doable. Also, it's probably a good idea to put your friend on an Information Diet for the foreseeable future. Be very selective and deliberate about what you do share.

THE HOW AND WHEN OF GIVING ADVICE

When you go out to eat at a restaurant, your server might ask you if you've dined with them before. If you have, they don't need to explain the menu, telling you what you already know and essentially wasting your time when you could be stuffing food into your face. This is common courtesy in a restaurant, and it should be common courtesy in friendships, too: Only give advice when it's wanted or has been requested. If you are the typical advice-giving type, we get it! You're coming from a good place! You just want to help! But pause to consider how your advice is being received: You may be accidentally talking down to someone you care about, or you might just be making your friends feel plain silly.

(You can safely assume that your friend has done all the obvious stuff. They probably already googled their problem and read the first ten results.)

One of Jenn's closest friends is a doctor, so Jenn sends her questions all the time, complete with gross photos: "Are my lymph nodes swollen? Is this bruise concerning?" They have an understanding that Jenn wants to hear what she thinks. If you don't have that type of agreement with your friend, do not launch right into what you think your friend should do after they share a dilemma with you. Assess the situation first. Let's say your friend told you, "I had such a bad day at work.

I gave a presentation, and it went poorly. I'm dreading work tomorrow." Your friend is simply issuing a complaint about their life. They are not necessarily seeking advice from you; they're expressing a frustration and need to hear from someone they trust, "Hey, that sucks, and I'm sorry." Avoid responses that sound like this:

- *Did you practice your presentation? Always practice presentations before giving them.* You are their friend. You are not their personal life coach, parent, or manager.
- *I've done a lot of public speaking—let me give you some tips for next time.* They probably already know what they need to improve and don't need to hear it again, especially from a pal.

- *You should speak with your boss about what happened.* This advice relies completely on assumption. You don't know the workplace dynamics—your friend does, which means they're the one who best understands the situation.

Consider responses that sound more like this:

- *That really sucks. I hope tomorrow will be better for you.*
- *I'm sorry you had a bad day. If you need to vent some more, I'm all ears.*
- *Do you want to vent, or do you want to talk about what to do next? I am up for either.*

Dear Friendshipping,

My friend is about to quit her job to do freelance photography full-time. She's getting her business off the ground and drafting agreements and contracts to give potential clients. I am not a lawyer or anything, but I have lots of experience because I run a small business myself. Is it weird if I invite myself to help her with this? Clients have taken advantage of her in the past, and I think I would be able to prevent that.

You have relevant expertise and experience, and you have the ability to help your friend with something important. This is an appropriate time to offer help. Don't insert yourself into their work (and probably avoid mentioning the bad client stuff from the past), but do lay out what you can provide. Be encouraging and clear: "So excited to see you go freelance! Would you be interested in seeing my boilerplate drafting agreement? I was just thinking that I wish I'd had that when I was starting out." If only everyone had a Paperwork Angel to visit them in times of need!

- *I've also done poorly on work presentations before. Let me know if you want my thoughts on moving on from this.*
- *I'm here for you if you want to have a soundboard for problem-solving, or if you just need someone to be angry on your behalf. I can do both or either.*

Essentially, you're asking for explicit permission before sounding off, and you are giving your friend some options for how the conversation can unfold. They are the one experiencing the bad day, so they are allowed to decide how the problem is discussed and managed. They are the protagonist, and you are not an expert on their subject. (Unless you are an actual expert! In which case, still ask permission before giving your advice, because your friend might be seeking you out only as a voice of support.)

Once you've gotten the go-ahead to advise your friend, here are some ways to buffer that advice:

- *What [methods / solutions / ideas] have you already tried?*
- *I've gotten good at [reading contracts / editing résumés / proofreading important emails], so let me know if you need another pair of eyes.*
- *Let's start with the basics, because I'll feel like a bonehead if I don't say it out loud: Did you try [obvious thing]?*
- *Let's talk this through. What do you think are the next steps?*
- *I've got a few thoughts on your situation. Let me know if now is a good time for them.*
- *Here's what I think, but of course, you know best here.*

INTERVENING WHEN YOU THINK YOUR FRIEND IS MAKING A HUGE MISTAKE

At some point, you will inevitably find yourself annoyed, alarmed, fearful, confused, or worried about your friends and their choices. (Let's be real: This has probably happened already.) Your friends will do something that makes you want to yell, "No no noooo, whyyyy why why?!" This is a tricky situation to navigate: What's your role here, exactly? You're caught between these two convictions:

Friends hold one another accountable for their actions. You can and should tell your friends when they're being harmful to themselves. You can be both a supportive friend and an honest friend.

And:

Your friends are fully grown adults living their imperfect lives just like everyone else, and you shouldn't police their behavior. Mind your own beeswax.

There's no clear answer. If your friends are being ridiculous, that is, in fact, a choice they are entitled to make. On the other hand, you certainly don't need to automatically endorse everything they do, and when you stay silent, you may be doing just that. If you've got a friend who is seriously worrying you, you have some questions to mull over:

IS YOUR ADVICE CONSIDERED NEW INFORMATION? What about helpful? Productive? If you've got a friend who chain-smokes cigarettes, they already know that smoking is unhealthy. This is common knowledge. You are not the genius who will inform them of this fact, and your interference will count for very little. (You are allowed to request that they don't smoke near you. That's a totally reasonable boundary to set. You just can't make anyone do anything, and that includes quitting smoking.)

HOW CLOSE ARE YOU, *REALLY*? Figure out how well you truly know each other. Assess the depth of your relationship. Social circles vary dramatically in this way. Some close friends feel like hand-picked members of your family; others you know quite well, but only see in the workplace; other people are friendly acquaintances you never speak with outside your morning commute. Have you two ever had a private conversation (before the one you're considering)? Has this person ever asked you for your advice or confided in you? Do you hang out one-on-one fairly often? In turn, how much private information do they know about you? If you are not that close, voicing your personal concerns might be off-putting, even inappropriate. They have other people in their life to talk to them about the serious stuff.

HAVE YOU CONSULTED WITH OTHER PEOPLE? You can mention what you've observed to other trusted friends, share your dilemma, and see what they think. It's not gossiping if you have real concerns! Something like, "My coworker is going through a divorce. Do you think I should send

an email to check in, or just give them space and privacy? What would you like, if it were you?" Or if your friend(s) knows the person: "I'm feeling worried about Ayesha. She's posting some concerning stuff on Instagram. Have you spoken with her about this before?" Enter the information-gathering phase before proceeding.

If you've considered these questions and you feel in your heart that something is very wrong, now is the time to speak up. This might be an easy task or an impossible-sounding one. Some friends have an established rapport that allows for total honesty. In college, when Jenn lived with two roommates she was close with, they would speak bluntly and with good humor. When her roommate was sleeping with a guy who was a bit of a jerk, Jenn would say, "I think that guy sucks and every time he leaves, you become miserable all over again," and her roommate would reply, "Yep, I know that!" and then still see him that night. And that was that. Jenn said her piece; the roommate said hers. It was an airing of grievances of sorts. Does that sound like a convo you could have? Maybe not. You might need to do more setup to ease you both into

Dear Friendshipping,

I'm pretty sure my friend is getting involved in one of those multi-level marketing schemes. Ugh. I really don't want to be judgmental about this—I have a job with a decent salary, and my friend currently does not—but I can't stand to see them spend time and effort (and their own money!) on what I'm pretty sure is a scam! At what point is it OK for me to bring this up?

First, take a deep breath, and redirect your anger and frustration to the source of the problem: the MLM that ensnared your friend. Isn't it awful that businesses are allowed to manipulate people in this way? Do your damnedest to summon empathy for your pal here, and if you decide to talk to your friend, begin with questions. "How's the new job going?" is a good start. "How do you like it?" "Is it going well?" Get a feel for where they're actually coming from. Are they stoked about selling protein shakes / knives / jewelry? Or are they fully aware that this sucks, and they don't have any other options? Remember: You are on your friend's team.

a serious conversation, like "I know we usually keep things light, which I love about us, but I do need to discuss something more serious with you." Or "Friend, I have bad news and good news. The bad news is I have to have an uncomfortable conversation with you. The good news: It will be over in five minutes."

You may get only one chance to do this, and there is no "undo" or "reset" button. Make it clear you are coming from a place of concern. Plan what you'll say and how you'll go about it, and know that this is your last attempt to meddle. Here are some scripts:

- *So here's the thing. I'm worried about you, and here's why.*
- *I just have to say it once: Is this the right time for you to jump into a new marriage?*
- *As your friend who loves you, I owe you my total honesty: I think sleeping with your intern is a terrible idea.*

Hopefully, you started a productive, if difficult, conversation with your friend. Or maybe your friend is still intent on making a decision that blows their life up (or at least gives you deep and abiding second-hand embarrassment). If you need to go nuclear, here are some ways to permanently get off the topic:

- *Let the record show that I support you as a friend and human being, but I do not support this choice.*
- *I appreciate you at least hearing me out. I need some time away from this subject.*
- *Friend, from here on out, talk to me about literally anything else in your life. Describe your PAP smear in vivid detail. Read me the ten-thousand-word backstory of your Blades in the Dark character. Anything.*

Side note: If the issue is related directly to your friend's health or body, you should either a) shut up, or b) be incredibly mindful and sensitive. You are not their physician, they are not your patient, and you do not have access to their medical or family history (and besides, actual doctors are often inconsiderate and get things wrong all the time). Is this a subject you can truly discuss with both authority and grace? You are an imperfect person laden with biases and judgments—as is everyone. Make sure that their behavior is alarming enough to bring up (which still doesn't mean you should, by the way), not just, like, annoying you. For example, if you're irked that your friend sleeps until noon and skips morning spin class every Saturday, that's your problem to deal with internally, not theirs. Why does this bother you? What's the actual source of your annoyance? Metathink this through, with the knowledge that your opinion on exercising is influenced by advertising, Western standards of beauty, how you were raised, where you were raised, and a dozen other factors. When it comes down to it, you are just being judgmental. Everybody makes judgments about other people, and that doesn't make you a bad person, but it's up to you to work on yourself and curb the voice in your head. It's not the role of a friend to determine when, how, and if someone else exercises, and it's inappropriate if that is consistently a "concern" of yours.

On the other hand, what if your friend is skipping their regular spin class and they're acting very differently, like showing signs of depression? What if they are consistently absent in class and work, playing addictive video games for hours each day, and neglecting to answer emails and texts from everybody? If you notice sudden changes in your friend's behavior or health, you can, in fact, check on them. This is what friends do for each other. You do not have to be the great solver of their problems, and you aren't going to make diagnoses, comment on their body or appearance or work ethic, speculate wildly, or dig into their complex psyche. You only have to say what you have personally observed. You can be the supportive person who says, "I noticed this, it feels to me like something is going on, and I'm in your corner." Like this:

- *Listen, I don't care if you ever go to the gym, but you've seemed pretty down for the last month, and we missed you at spin again. How are you?*
- *You've missed labs and classes lately, and it's just not like you to be this absent. What's up? You need a listening ear?*
- *I've known you for a long time, Friend, and this just doesn't seem normal for you.*
- *This is not my area of expertise, but what I can do is [join you on a walk / take you out for dinner / make you breakfast / bring over a box of donuts] and listen.*
- *Hey, was it just me, or were you having a hard time at the barbecue on Sunday? You don't have to spill anything you don't want to share right now. This is just me checking in on you!*
- *I noticed you haven't been popping up in the group chat. We missed you at movie night last week, too. Everything OK?*
- *I love you a lot and I would be angry with myself if I didn't make this suggestion: I think seeing a counselor could help you out.*
- *I admit that I have been feeling worried about you. Have you ever thought about seeing a professional?*

Notice that these examples do not include the word "should." *You should go to therapy! You should clean your apartment! You should do yoga!* Telling a stressed or depressive person that they should do yoga is about as helpful and effective as punching them in the face.

WHEN YOU'RE THE ONE GETTING ADVICE

Look, receiving unsolicited advice is incredibly annoying, but we are going to advocate for it just for a second here: Sometimes your friends give you advice because they have weighed the options and decided it's worth being annoying for a few seconds in order to earnestly help you in the long run. Close friends can act as an early alert system for personal disasters. People who love you and know you well have a sense of what your "normal" looks like, so they can detect when there's a change and something's gone off the rails. That's why it's important to take things seriously if a bunch of your loved ones give you the same advice.

On the other hand, you certainly don't need to follow all the advice you're given. You don't need to leave every aspect of your life open to feedback. Do you have a friend who gives you advice constantly? Ugh. Well, let's consider this from their point of view for a moment. They assume when you share your problems aloud, you are seeking their help and input. Your friendship = autopermission to give their thoughts. Eager and especially helpful people—the Leslie Knopes of the world— have a hard time recognizing that this isn't always the case. It's time to clue them in. You can absolutely give them a polite nudge that says, "Back off with the advice, please, thanks." Here are some scripts for the next time your friend gets all fixy:

- *Thanks for your concern. I'll keep that in mind! I'm not looking for further advice right now.*
- *I was just venting, not looking for answers yet. Thanks anyway.*
- *I appreciate your input, but I got this one.*

You can even get ahead of the problem and say exactly what you are looking for. Like so:

- *My problem is [detailed right here]. By the way, not looking for advice on this. Just had to tell someone.*
- *Can I vent for a second? Disclaimer: I don't need input or advice, just a listening ear.*

It's a little hokey, but you're essentially telling your friends/loved ones how you prefer to be treated and how to love you properly. And if this doesn't work? From now on, you need to share your problems with a different friend altogether.

One last note here: We have to address the worst and most uncharitable possibility. Is your friend being disrespectful or intrusive? If your friend is belittling, frequently talks down to you, and instructs you how to live your life, that's not a friend. That's a bully. Or a really crappy babysitter. You don't need either of those in your life.

RESPECTING YOURSELF, RESPECTING YOUR FRIENDS

ESTABLISHING BOUNDARIES

Friends support one another. Friends help bear one another's burdens in life. But look, you have limits. Everyone does! You're not inconsiderate for feeling unable to devote unlimited quantities of time to a friend. If you can offer a listening ear to people in distress, that's a wonderful gift to give. But it's a gift—not a role that you take on for life. Most importantly, you are not your friend's doctor, counselor, or therapist. If you are not an electrician, you wouldn't take apart your friend's circuit breaker.

If you are not a plumber, you would not idly tinker with your main water line. When we tell you that being your friend's permanent sounding board is not your job, we mean it.

If your friend unloads on you, it's because you keep responding. So it's time to change your habits and establish new boundaries. What can you offer instead? Consider what you can and cannot give. Be completely realistic and honest with yourself regarding your abilities, your schedule, and your attention level. You *can't* pick up the phone at midnight any longer, but you *can* drop a meal off at your friend's door on your way home from work. You *can't* answer a dozen messages during the workday, but you *can* send a quick text over your lunch break to say they are on your mind. You are creating a courteous boundary for yourself and putting an understandable limit on your time, like this:

- *I know we've been talking during the workday, but I realized that I probably shouldn't pick up the phone while I'm at work unless it's an emergency. I want to be there for you, so let's find another time to talk.*
- *So I decided I'm setting a new curfew for myself. In fifteen minutes, I need to get offline and study. Until then, keep talking—I am here to listen.*
- *Heads up: I'm turning off my phone at 11:00 p.m. so I can get some shut-eye.*
- *I need some time to myself tonight, so let's reschedule for next week. Hope you had a better day today.*

Then, stick to your guns. Hold fast to the boundaries you have set and try not to feel guilty (easier said than done, we know). You are not being mean—you are being genuine with both yourself and your friend. It is not impolite to state what you need.

VENT WITH CONSENT!

Venting is good for you! And it's so, so normal among friends, but it can't be one-sided or excessive (then it's not venting; it's just dumping your problems onto someone without consent). Here's how to keep yourself in check:

ASK FOR THEIR TIME. Before you dive into what's bothering you, begin with something like "I need to kvetch, do you mind if I vent for five minutes?" Or "Are you free tonight? I could use some career advice, so let me know when it's OK to give you a call." This shows you are respecting their time and what they do for you.

DO UNTO OTHERS. Have you asked your friend lately how *they* are doing (and listened intently to hear their answer)? If you are unloading on your friend every single day and doing nothing else together, you're not treating your friend as your friend, you're treating them as a stand-in for a mental health professional.

SHOW GRATITUDE. When your friend puts their life on hold to help you with your problems, they are giving you the gift of their time. Time is not something anyone can get back. Get in the habit of winding down the conversation by offering something like, "As always, I appreciate your wisdom," or "Thank you for allowing me to gripe." Or even: "Is there anything YOU need to complain about? I am happy to listen!"

On the other hand, establishing limits may not fix the problem. Your friend could completely disregard the parameters you've attempted to set. People are not always adept at following social cues, *especially* social cues that they don't like, *especially* when they are deep in the trenches of bad feelings. If this happens, it may be that you have to stop being their go-to person altogether. We are not suggesting that you go cold turkey here and cut them off and abruptly ignore them—that's a drastic change for both of you—but you can (gently and firmly) pull away from being your friend's personal therapist and point them toward more constructive resources for managing their problems. You can be blunt, you can be funny, whatever feels right for the tone of the conversation, but be as clear as possible. Use your own words, but here are some scripts you can work from:

- *So listen, I can't help ya with your dating problems anymore. Every time you ask me for advice about women from here on out, you have to pay me $5. Deal?*
- *Let's brainstorm some ideas for better help and resources.*
- *I wish I could help, but I've realized that I'm totally unequipped for this one. Have you given any thought to talking with a counselor?*
- *I'm out of my depth. I wish I had advice to give. What I can do is have you over soon to distract you with a romantic comedy. Do you feel up to getting out this weekend?*

The most important part is explaining that you are *making a change* in how your friendship operates. Before, you were the person your friend could vent to all the time. Going forward, you are not going to be this person. The dynamic is going to morph into something new, and you'll have to be very clear about how. From now on, you'll be the distraction who invites them over to watch a crappy movie, or the helpful friend who walks their dog when they work late, or the optimistic cheerleader as they search for therapists.

Or maybe you want to take on none of these roles, and that is absolutely OK. ("I'm not the right person to help you with this" or "Friend, I love ya, but I need to officially bow out of this [convo / subject / problem]."") Even if your friend is unwell or sad or not neurotypical,

they are still an adult with the ability to make choices on how they treat you. Whether you no longer want to be part of your friend's life in this way or you tried setting a boundary and your friend is still pounding on your door—literally or figuratively—you will have to be firmer and more direct than you have been before. (We're very sorry that the bulk of this work falls to you.) If the situation does become dire, here are some ways to speak up:

- *I need you to value my time. I told you that sending me so many emails is not working for me. From now on, I am not going to look at those messages. If you need to reach me, here's how.*
- *I can't manage your divorce with you anymore, and as I said, I need a long break from talking about it. Please respect that.*
- *We need to speak about boundaries. I know you are going through a rough time, but as I said before, I can't field daily phone calls any longer. Please stop calling me.*
- *This subject is now off-limits.*

Dear Friendshipping,

My friend comes over a few times a week. She doesn't get along with her roommates and finds it comforting to come to my place to chat and vent. Unfortunately, I can't get her out of my house! I go to bed early, and she doesn't; she wants to stay up and ask me for advice on every roommate situation. It's hard for me to keep hosting her late at night. How do I deal?

It's very thoughtful that you are offering a friend a safe haven while she endures an unhappy living situation. While you are kind to your friend, you should be kind to yourself, too, and that means advocating for your needs, like a good night's sleep! Sleep is mandatory. How do you think your friend might feel if she knew she was cutting into something so essential? It's time to let her know how to be a good friend in return. You can say, "Hey, Friend, I'm exhausted, time to kick you out now!" Or "You know me: I need to get to bed by midnight, or I'm a mess the next day." Or "Let's stick to hanging out on the weekends so I have more energy." You can also hang out at neutral locations only—coffee shops, a restaurant, the park, their back porch. Then you can leave whenever you want. (And fingers crossed that this whole thing is temporary; we hope that your friend is able to find new roommates or a new place to live soon.)

What this person does next is not your responsibility. If they are angry, let them have their anger. If they are confused, let them sit in their confusion. They may argue, they may say they are hurt, they may try to convince you that you're being mean. But you are more than what you can do for other people. You do not exist to be the dumping ground for the issues of others. You have a complete life of your own that deserves your attention. We truly believe in giving your time and your support to your friends, but not when doing so is draining you of life.

SO YOU THINK *YOU* MIGHT BE AN ASSHOLE

Everyone acts like an asshole sometimes. If you're starting to recognize that your friends are drawing more and more boundaries with you, it may be time for some self-reflection. Self-reflection means looking critically at your actions, habits, and behaviors. It means staring directly at the proof you are ignoring and considering the very real consequences of your actions. To get a little closer to understanding yourself, here are some questions to meditate on (and not just gloss over). This is not a yes or no checklist or a definitive test of whether you are kind or not. We don't know if you are an asshole. Honestly, you might be one. It's not like they are rare in the world. But being an asshole is not a permanent role that you must play for life. You can shed your asshole behaviors. First, let's see if *you* can recognize what they are. Begin by asking yourself:

DO I MAKE AN EFFORT TO PUT OTHER PEOPLE AT EASE? It's so much easier to be polite when you're well rested and everything is perfect. But humans and situations rarely feel perfect! We have to go to busy airports and sit through long meetings that really should be emails. When you are annoyed, inconvenienced, pressed for time, exhausted,

CHECK YOUR MEDIA INTAKE

One way to examine and change your biases? Look at the media you consume. Make sure you are going out of your way to watch, read, and listen to content made by people who span all race, gender, ability, and age profiles. This isn't a perfect suggestion—there is no standard experience for every individual in a marginalized group, and this will not make you an expert. Understanding how to treat people well is a lifelong experience, but you can begin to learn from people who experience the world differently from you on a daily basis.

or hangry, what's your tone of voice? How about when you are speaking with your flight attendant, office admin, or cab driver? These are tests of your everyday character.

WHAT ARE MY BIASES? We live in an unequal world. People punish and reward others based on their race, income, sexuality, age, ability, appearance, gender, and countless other reasons. It's not your fault that society is built this way, but you do have to unlearn (and keep unlearning) prejudices that you've been poisoned with. If your friend group is completely homogenous, for example, that's worth reflection. Don't suddenly attempt to make friends of every flavor, but consider how you can adjust your behavior to be more welcoming to people who are different from you. You are responsible for your counterprogramming.

IN WHAT KIND OF SITUATIONS DO I TAKE CREDIT? REVERSELY, WHEN DO I TAKE THE BLAME? Assholes rarely, if ever, take accountability when a situation goes poorly, but always give themselves credit when things go well. Do you take time to reflect on how your own choices and behavior alter outcomes?

HOW DO I FEEL WHEN PEOPLE TELL ME NO? AND WHAT DO I SAY IN RESPONSE? When a rejection feels hurtful, what really matters is how you act. Do you begin negotiating? Are you accepting? Are you somewhere in between? Do you ask clearly for what you need, or do you demand what you want?

ARE MY FRIENDS JERKS? You are the company you keep. You get to choose who you spend your time with, and you may be choosing jerks. The behavior of your friends reflects on you. Even if you don't personally agree with some of the shitty things your friends say and do, you are endorsing their behavior when you stand by them.

WHO'S LAUGHING AT MY JOKES? What groups of people benefit from your jokes, and what groups are hurt by them? Take notice of what your comedy is really about and who it is intended for.

IS YELLING A COMMON OCCURRENCE? Screaming at people is not normal in relationships. It's so rarely the correct way to manage conflict. Do you antagonize people in the hopes that they will lose their cool? How often do you deliberately play devil's advocate?

WHEN WAS THE LAST TIME I SAID "I'M SORRY" AFTER A FIGHT, MISTAKE, OR ACCIDENT? Everyone makes mistakes. Not everyone apologizes. What tone of voice did you use when you apologized? Was your apology accepted?

DO I CLEAN UP AFTER MYSELF? We mean this question literally, especially if you share a living or workspace. Do you know where the cleaning supplies are stored? How often do you reach for them?

Did any of those questions particularly resonate? Did you skim past a few because you didn't like how they made you feel? Maybe you had no reaction at all. Point blank: If you are often unhappy with yourself, your behavior, or your relationships, you can (and should) work on yourself to become kinder and lighter and yep now here's where we recommend going to therapy. (You must have known this was coming eventually!) If it's accessible to you, finding a therapist you trust—and then making yourself go to the sessions and truly putting in the time—is always our most enthusiastic recommendation to combat loss, anxiety, or feelings of worthlessness or hopelessness. Therapy is not just paying a stranger to ask, "So why do you feel that way?" and crying on a leather couch. A good therapist can:

- Challenge the assumptions you have about yourself and the world
- Call you on your bullshit
- Discuss how early life experiences may have shaped you
- Point to patterns in your thinking and in your behavior
- Allow you to safely say something aloud that you would never say to another person
- Allow you to get to know yourself and understand what makes you react to certain situations
- Help manage stress, anger, grief, and trauma, or big unanswerable questions you have about life
- Recognize patterns in the people you seek out and in the people you avoid
- Help you through the end of a relationship, job loss, or other major life change
- Improve how you communicate and share your thoughts
- Clarify how you see yourself and others

The first time Jenn walked into a therapist's office, the therapist introduced herself and explained that while they were in the room together, "[Jenn] was allowed to yell, cry, swear, and throw things—just not at [her]." She established that the space was safe and private—a place to unbury emotions and get ugly. Not that you have to be particularly emotional or sensitive to go to therapy. You don't have to be crumpled and sobbing on the floor, either. You can seek it out simply because you feel curious, want to get to know yourself better, or suspect that your life could be easier.

If you can and want to give therapy a try, here's what we would like you to know:

PATIENCE IS REQUIRED. Your first few sessions may feel like a total waste of effort. It's a type of treatment, and treatment takes time. Pretend it's like *physical* therapy, which typically unfolds over many months. Attend a handful of sessions before you decide it isn't working. **YOU'LL WANT TO LIE.** It took Jenn weeks and weeks to work up the courage to speak openly. She wanted to either exaggerate tremendously to make her therapist laugh (who doesn't love an audience?) or to completely downplay her feelings.

Dear Friendshipping,

I'm not a shy person. I consider myself pretty outgoing. And yet my friend groups tend to hang out without me or break up eventually because of some drama or other. Is there something wrong with the way I am treating people?

We get questions like this all the time. It's a common worry. Our short answer: Maybe! Our longer answer: There certainly could be something wrong with how you treat people. You've noticed an unfortunate pattern in your broken friendships, but awareness is the first step toward making changes. Good job! So something needs to be reworked. What is it? Here are some possibilities: Do you tend to gravitate toward people who need to be won over? Are you flaky with plans? Could you put more energy into socializing? Are you making the effort that you want your friends to make for you? It could be that your friends adore you, but *you* don't like you very much, so you view their love through a distorted lens.

Regardless, even very nice people can have poor habits, or behave in ways that they have no idea are offensive to other people. Before you force yourself to wear a huge scarlet A for Asshole, look at the things you can change: your own behavior, your own perspective, whom you choose to spend time with. Control the controllables, take a critical look at yourself and your friendships, that everyone needs to make changes throughout their lives. It's called growth, and we all gotta go through it.

YOU MIGHT CRY. Like, a lot! And it might startle or surprise you. But crying unexpectedly is likely your body's way of signaling that you have reached an important topic. You may have just touched a wound you didn't know you had. Luckily, most therapists supply tissues.

THERAPISTS ARE HUMANS, TOO. That means they are susceptible to bad days, off days, illnesses, mistakes, judgment errors, and being bad at their jobs. (Trin, who is bisexual, once visited a therapist who did not believe that people could be bisexual.) You may not find the right therapist on your first go. If that's the case, we don't recommend writing off therapy completely; give another therapist a try. (And this will involve an annoying series of tasks: emails, phone calls, schedules, insurance, paperwork. Stay the course as best you can.)

GO EASY ON YOURSELF. Try not to worry about how much progress you're making or if you're saying the correct things. Many of us want to be impressive and do well in therapy, but there are no tests or grades. Actually, scratch that. There *are* grades for therapy, and we're giving you an A+ just for trying. Gold star, even. Good job.

Unfortunately, we know, therapy is not easily accessible. Some therapists offer fees on a sliding income scale, but it can still be pretty

What We Wish We'd KNOWN ABOUT THERAPY

- A clock will be in the room, and your therapist will likely tell you when time is almost up.

- You can bring stuff along to sessions—notes, journals, emails, text messages, reminders, calendars.

- Some therapists will hold sessions over the phone or video chat if needed.

- There may be silences. It will feel awkward. It's an awkward relationship! This is a stranger you're telling personal things to! (It does tend to get easier.)

- Your therapist might recommend you start seeing someone else. That's not a dig against you. They just want you to have the right fit.

- Sometimes, you will dislike your therapist. They will almost certainly ask you stuff you don't want to think about (which is kind of the point).

118

costly. Therapy requires time, money, transportation, energy—maybe a babysitter, or time away from work. (Also patience, motivation, and an open mind.) That's a lot to ask. Therapy might not be right for you. Regardless, there is no wrong time to seek the help you need; it's never too late nor too early. And even if you cannot seek therapy, you *can* create space and time to confront your emotions. Find an outlet to freely and safely unburden yourself. Online communities, in-person communities, support groups, hotlines, self-help books, journaling—there are always ways to get the help you need.

THE ART OF APOLOGIES

Apologizing is one of the most essential rituals of adulthood. Or at least it should be, because everyone hurts the people they care about; it's an unfortunate and inevitable consequence of being a human rather than a robot. Sometimes you will make the best decision you can with the information you have, and that choice will have consequences that hurt people. Sometimes you will flat-out screw up. A good apology is a promise to do better and to hold yourself accountable for it.

Of course, even the most heartfelt and eloquent apology may not be enough in some situations. We can't guarantee that your apology will earn acceptance or even deserve acceptance. That's up to the injured party to decide. (We'll get into that, too.) But how you handle the aftermath of hurting someone reveals your character and integrity, so we want you to learn how to clean up properly when you make mistakes.

APOLOGIZING FOR A RECENT MISTAKE

If you've recently hurt a friend, first reflect on what happened and decide how you are going to move forward from the mistake. If this is an oil spill, how are you going to contain the breach and prevent further damage? What's going to be different now—how are you going to change? To be clear, we're not referring to the smallish accidents, like forgetting to drop a card in the mail, not returning a routine phone call, or failing to give back the charger you borrowed. Everyone shits the bed a little. We're talking about the moments when you've truly caused harm. In these cases, you gotta internalize the change you hope to make. *Then* you can talk to your friend.

Carefully consider how you'll bring up the issue. Are you going to write an email? Ask for a few minutes of their time and stop by their place? Send a basket of cookies? Your apology should not be disruptive; it has to be timed to their schedule. Apologies can be sweet and funny—like a big ugly "I'm sorry" balloon delivered to their door—but you don't want to come across as trivial or infantilizing. A gift may imply that you are skirting the real issues when what you need to do is take responsibility. Imagine what your friend truly wants here.

A sincere and impactful apology:

DOESN'T ASK FOR ANYTHING IN RETURN. Whether or not they choose to extend forgiveness to you is for them to decide.

IS NOT YOUR TIME TO DECIDE HOW ANGRY OR UPSET YOUR FRIEND SHOULD BE. Don't say, "Please don't be too mad at me." It's not your place to set the terms.

IS SPECIFIC AND ACTIVE. You did the thing, so own up to it. Instead of "I'm sorry if you are upset about your broken hot tub," try "I'm sorry I broke your hot tub. I should have read the instructions before operating."

SHOULD NOT BE A LENGTHY MONOLOGUE. When you're over-explaining what you did and why you did it, you are likely justifying your behavior.

Here are examples of apologies that feel awful to receive:

- *Are you mad at me for what I said about your accent? I feel weird about it. Are we cool? Can we just forget it?*
- *Sorry I missed your birthday dinner, but I've been so busy with work lately. You didn't send a reminder email, so you can't be too mad!*
- *Oops, I got your pronouns mixed up. It's really hard for me to remember them! Honestly, I'll probably screw up a few more times.*

Here are muuuuch better apologies:

- *Friend, I need to apologize for what I said the other day. I'm sorry I made that comment about your accent. I crossed the line.*
- *I'm sorry I didn't come to your birthday dinner, especially because I said I would be there. Please know that this was a complete mistake on my part, and no indication of how much I love you, which is a whole lot. I would love to take you to dinner soon.*
- *Friend, I realized that I got your pronouns incorrect when I introduced you to my coworkers yesterday. I'm sorry.*

One solid apology is all you need to deliver—no need to take up more of your friend's time. After that, it's time to back off. Give your friend space to absorb what you said. No groveling. No follow-up messages. This is out of your hands now.

WHEN THE APOLOGY IS OVERDUE

Can you apologize for something you did years and years ago? We hear this question all the time. People want encouragement or permission to reach out to a person that they wronged in, say, high school, or in their early twenties, or when they were a kid. We get it. You still feel pangs of sadness and guilt. You want to apply a new bandage to an old wound and move on with your life. But apologies are not always the fix-all that we hope for.

At this point, your apology is outdated and overdue, so the kindest and most generous act might be simply leaving the person you hurt in peace. We won't tell you to *never* give this type of long-awaited apology, but we are going to insist that before you do it, you think it through long and hard. Ask yourself *who* the apology is really for. Is it for the person who was wronged—or is it for yourself? Are you trying to relieve yourself of guilt? Because there are other ways to work through consistent feelings of guilt (therapy, anyone?) that do not involve contacting the person you hurt. What are you hoping to get out of this apology? Their forgiveness? Because there's no guarantee you'll even get a response, let alone their forgiveness. Keep in mind that you are going to surprise this person and possibly disrupt their life.

Before you reach out, do this exercise: Write down the apology you want to say, the one that is weighing heavily on your heart. Express your regrets. Get it all out. And then, don't deliver it. Writing the apology—and the promise that you will do better in the future and try harder—might be exactly what you need to free yourself up emotionally. And keep this quote close to your heart: "The best apology is changed behavior."

ACCEPTING AND REJECTING APOLOGIES

When someone hurts you, it's up to you to decide how to move forward. Receiving apologies is its own complicated emotional mess. Because humans can't be expected to do the right thing all the time, forgiveness is central to any long-term friendship. It is wonderful when friends can make amends and move on with their lives. But you don't have to auto-accept an apology just because you received one. You may feel pressured to be "cool" about it, not make a big deal out of things, or turn the other cheek. But you have more options than you may realize:

YOU CAN ACCEPT AN APOLOGY BUT STILL FEEL HURT AND NOT FORGIVE THAT PERSON. In this case, you are neutralizing the situation, which might be for the best if it brings you peace. This is a good option if you believe the apologizer to be volatile and you need some space. This usually isn't the best option if you have a loving relationship with the apologizer, because it may require you to rehash the situation later on and pull back that faux-acceptance.

YOU CAN ACCEPT AN APOLOGY EARNESTLY AND THEN PUT DISTANCE BETWEEN YOU BOTH. You might even forgive someone and want to continue your friendship, but what they did was too painful, and now you can only associate them with that pain. This happens! It's not a sign that you need to force yourself to let them back into your life. Distance can be best for both parties, and it can also be temporary.

YOU CAN FORGIVE BUT NOT FORGET. "Forgiving but not forgetting" sounds way more dramatic than it is. You can accept that a person no longer owes you anything for having wronged you, while simultaneously putting up some barriers to protect yourself in the future. You're withdrawing some of your trust, temporarily or perhaps permanently.

YOU CAN REJECT THE APOLOGY. Before you do, ask yourself: *Did this person accept responsibility? Did they show genuine remorse? What is it that would make me feel better? Can I think of anything? Do I believe that their behavior can and will change?* (The answer might be no!) Rejecting an apology can be devastating for both you and your friend, so treat this situation with as much thought and care as you can manage.

HOW TO ASK FOR AN APOLOGY

Your friends—even your dearest and nearest and most beloved friends—are imperfect people. You, too, are an imperfect person. If a friend has hurt you, and you're not sure what to do about it, first consider that:

- You've made mistakes before. You've taken the easy way out or failed to listen.
- You have been selfish and unkind, and you've said the exact wrong thing at the exact wrong time.
- You've said things that are hurtful. You've excluded people based on your internalized, societally trained ideas of who is worthy of inclusion and who isn't.
- You have made people feel sad and you have made people feel unwelcome.

Everything on this list is true of every person who has ever lived. We are telling you this not to make you feel bad, but so you remember that no one will do right by you every second of their life. You should have high standards for friends, but those standards should also be realistic and allow people to be people. Those standards apply to you, too. You can let some mistakes go; this is what friends do for one another, and certainly something that has been done for you.

So how do you know if you should speak up or let things go? There's no obvious right or wrong answer, but it's probably time to speak up if:

- You feel that you are nursing a wound that will fester with time, instead of heal with time. (Never mind the cliché—time does not actually heal all wounds.)
- You can't picture ever having fun with your friend again without first having a serious conversation or receiving an apology.
- You can't relax or laugh when this friend is present or on your mind.
- You believe that your friend will continue to hurt you in this way.

You deserve to be treated with respect and kindness, and you have every right to advocate for yourself. So let's say you are going to speak up. (Good for you.) It's possible your friend has absolutely no idea you are feeling hurt or that they made a mistake. Or maybe they have an inkling, but they don't know just *how* badly they messed up, or they are simply in denial. Here are some ways you can clue them in:

- *Last week you made a joke about my buzzcut. I didn't say anything at the time, but I've thought about it, and it's bothering me.*
- *Friend, this is uncomfortable for me to bring up, but I need to say it: I can't deal with the way you treat people during our kickball games. I can't be part of the team anymore unless there are major changes from you: no more raising your voice, no more confrontations with the umpire or opposing team.*
- *When you introduced me to your coworkers, you misgendered me repeatedly. I need you to notice your mistakes and do better.*

Include what happened and how you feel. If you can, add what you need to move forward from this. Maybe you want an explanation, or you just want your friend to know how you feel. Or maybe you require an apology. You can, in fact, ask for an apology—it's not unreasonable to want one. Regardless, be concise and clear here. You want your friend to understand you, and you don't want to inspire a debate over the events that transpired. (You can't debate someone's feelings.) So remove any unnecessary details—especially over email or text. Ten-paragraph emails so rarely lead to productive conversations.

We won't pretend this will be easy. It will suck! You'll probably feel awkward, especially if you've never done this before. But awkwardness doesn't mean that you shouldn't state your needs. You are giving your friend the opportunity to apologize and make necessary repairs to your friendship. That's a kindness for both of you. Advocating for yourself is one of the hardest, most grown-up things you can do.

How your friend responds will tell you how they handle conflict and uncomfortable conversations. This is valuable information, and it might not be information you like. We cannot promise that this conversation will go smoothly and everything will get resolved and you'll feel so much lighter afterward. If only. These are some of the possible unfortunate outcomes:

- You get an excellent, thoughtful apology—and you still don't feel better.
- Your friend gives an "apology" that is crappy and insincere and makes you feel worse.
- Your friend gives a crappy apology, but you decide to accept it anyway just to move on with your life.
- Your friend apologizes but doesn't change or edit their behavior at all.

- You get a great apology and feel relieved after getting this apology, but don't want to continue the friendship.
- Your friend doesn't apologize and instead tries to argue with you.
- Your friend feels so badly that they have a meltdown, and now it's unfairly your job to reassure *them*.

On the other hand, here are more positive outcomes:

- Your friend apologizes sincerely and edits their hurtful behavior.
- Your friend appreciates your honesty.
- Your friend is really relieved and grateful they have someone telling them how to be kinder.
- Things are awkward for the next few weeks, but then you both get back to normal.
- You're proud that you stuck up for yourself like the mature grown-up you are.
- You endure something difficult together, so this conversation actually brings you closer together.
- You come to realize that you need to wind down the friendship; you have other people in your life who treat you like you deserve.

Asking for apologies is not easy. But whether the outcome is good or bad, you've learned something meaningful about yourself, your friend, and your relationship. You can move on knowing that you gave someone you care about the opportunity to make things right.

PART THREE

On Keeping Friends
The Tricky Stuff

FAVORS IN FRIENDSHIP

ALL THE SMALL THINGS

Asking friends for favors can be pretty damn difficult. We often ask too little for ourselves yet worry that we are asking too much. But psychology studies say that asking for favors actually strengthens the bond between friends: It's a sign of trust and closeness, and it inspires positive feelings for both parties. People really do like helping people. (We know that might be difficult to believe.) So just in case no one has told you this before, we'll tell you now: It's OK to ask your friends for favors! Especially the small favors that add a little bit of sunshine to your day or make your week go more smoothly. We're all just trying to make life easier for one another, aren't we? Here's what to remember when you ask friends for help with the everyday stuff:

MEASURE BOTH SIDES OF THE FAVOR. Think about how much you are asking of your friend versus how much the favor would help you. Here's an example: You feel hesitant to ask a friend to drive you home from work on Friday because you've never done so before, and you're worried that you're a big ol' bother. But think about the logistics: Picking you up would take your friend just an additional ten minutes on their commute, and in turn, you would be able to make your kid's ballet recital on time. That's worth the ask!

BE DIRECT AND PERSONAL. Say what you need in one or two sentences and explain the impact of their help. "If you drove me, I would be able to make it to Aiden's ballet recital on time." Or "I would love to read that book for my long flight. Can I borrow it? If so, can you bring it to work tomorrow?" Or "Do you have a spare twenty minutes to edit my cover letter tonight? After that I will be ready to send it off!"

You Can Reasonably
ASK YOUR FRIENDS TO:

- Edit your résumé or cover letter
- Gently critique your outfit
- Give romantic or professional advice
- Rescue you from an awkward conversation or situation
- Pick you up or drop you off at the airport
- Pet-sit, babysit, house-sit, or plant-sit
- Meet you at the park, your apartment, or the bar after a rough day

- Go to a movie with you even though they don't want to see it
- Cover the cost of your coffee because you forgot your wallet
- Accompany you to a boring event you don't want to attend alone
- Act as a glowing reference for a job, pet, or apartment application
- Preview a difficult text message or email
- Fix your crappy Wi-Fi connection
- Help you move furniture
- Share your Kickstarter project / blog post / professional photography with their networks
- Borrow their KitchenAid mixer
- Drop meds and supplies at your doorstep when you're sick

OF COURSE, NO GUILT TRIPS. Don't assume you are going to get a yes just because you asked nicely. Before asking the favor, make sure you are willing to say earnestly, "That's totally OK! Thank you anyway!" Or "No problem, totally understand." Or "Well, now I'm so angry I could punch the sun," but you know, jokingly. Everyone has their own shit going on, and just because they couldn't find the time to proofread your cover letter doesn't mean they aren't supportive, loving, and crossing their fingers for you to get that job you want.

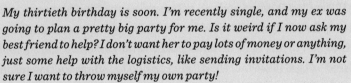

Dear Friendshipping,

My thirtieth birthday is soon. I'm recently single, and my ex was going to plan a pretty big party for me. Is it weird if I now ask my best friend to help? I don't want her to pay lots of money or anything, just some help with the logistics, like sending invitations. I'm not sure I want to throw myself my own party!

The way we see it, you've got two options:

1. **Throw your own party.** You can absolutely throw a party for yourself! If it makes you feel weird, you can place the focus on the hangout and not shine a spotlight on yourself; you can skip the cake or decor. But also, you *can* shine a spotlight on yourself! It's just one day, and you made it through another rotation around the sun. You are worth celebrating.

2. **Ask your friend to cohost.** Be extremely clear about what that means, exactly. You're looking for someone to be on your team: helping with the guest list, greeting people as they arrive, refilling drinks, making sure people are having a nice time, etc. You plan to handle expenses and major decisions, and you'd like someone to be your backup when the party starts.

WHEN THE ASK IS BIG

When you're asking for a larger, more time-consuming favor, be mind-blowingly clear about what you need (and usually why, depending on the circumstances), when you need it, and how you will try to repay the kindness in the future. Notice your tone if you're speaking and watch the words you use if you're typing. Make sure to use the word "please." (Even if you feel like you have already said "please," double check to make sure you actually did.) Here's an example of a considerate email:

> Hey, you!
>
> I'm heading out of town to see my sister's baby the first weekend of August. I know you said you would be up for taking care of my cat because of your vet experience, and I'd like to take you up on that! I'm wondering if you can please stay at my apartment for the two days I am gone.
>
> As you know, Sprocket needs special care. You'll have to express her bladder every twelve hours. I will give you a full demo beforehand. I know you've done this before with animals at your clinic, and yeah, it's a thing.
>
> And I'm totally fine with you having a few friends over. Sprocket loves company. I'll leave my credit card with you so you can order pizzas on me.
>
> Let me know what you think! Thank you!

We know that feels like a very specific email, but you should provide even the tiniest details that your friend may need in order to make a decision: the scope, the potential difficulties, the potential upsides, how available you will be, and everything else you can think of ahead of time. You are so familiar with taking care of your pet that you have internalized the thousand things you do for Sprocket each day. Look at this from another perspective and itemize what you are asking a friend to do, beginning to end. That list could look like: pack up their computer and clothes; drive to your house for a weekend; schedule their day around your pet; know how to reach your emergency veterinarian; repeatedly interact with your cat's butt.

If applicable, highlight how you plan to repay your friend for their time. Obviously, the larger / grosser / longer / more expensive the favor, the more you oughta repay them. If you find yourself writing paragraphs of instructions on Sprocket's bowels, you should translate that into a thoughtful gift for your friend, something they would enjoy and perhaps never ask for themselves, like this:

- *I know this is a big ask, and I would really appreciate you stepping in, if you can. I'm going to get a few pounds of your favorite coffee beans and leave them beside the French press for you. Have at it.*
- *I would like to pay you for your time. I'll give you $50 and stock the fridge with a variety of exciting cheeses.*
- *Before I leave, I'm going to buy you a copy of Animal Crossing because I know you've wanted to play it!*
- *I'll leave the passwords to HBO, Netflix, and Hulu, and get you a six-pack of your favorite beer. You can even sleep on the waterbed!*

Of course, you don't have to spend money in order to properly thank someone:

- *When I'm back in town, I will owe you a favor that you can keep in your back pocket until you need it.*
- *I know you have a month-long trip coming up in the fall, and I would be happy to feed your fish, get your mail, and water your plants while you are away.*
- *In turn, I will let you pick the next three movies we watch, no matter how terrible they are, and I will not complain once.*

A handwritten and heartfelt note can go a long way to making a friend feel loved and heard, too. Imagine how sweet it would be to get this in the mail: "Thank you for taking such good care of Sprocket last week. Having you there was an enormous relief, and a huge weight off my shoulders. I'm so lucky to have a friend like you." Aw, shucks!

By the way, it's important to be mindful of how often you ask for favors—not that there's a correct number here, exactly. There isn't a blanket policy that states "You may request from me three (3) favors total within a thirty-day period." But consider how often you are asking, and from whom. If you are repeatedly asking the same friend because you're super confident they'll always say yes, a power imbalance might be in play. You would never want to take advantage of anyone's kindness. It's important, too, that you don't make your friend say no more than once. Don't make a friend grapple for new ways to politely turn you down. Of course there's an answer you prefer more, but still: make saying no easy for friends to do.

WHY IT'S SO HARD FOR SOME PEOPLE TO ASK FOR HELP

If you are in a place of prolonged difficulty—you have a family member in the hospital, you were recently laid off from your job, you are grieving a loss, you've broken up with your partner—we hope that you are asking for more help than you usually would. Your friends *want* to help you. We want you to try to convince yourself of this fact, especially if you are not able to bring yourself to request, "Can you please drive my kids to school in the morning? I haven't slept more than three hours a night in a week." Or "I can't get off the couch. Can you please do me a favor and run to the pharmacy to pick up cold medicine?" Your hesitation is not unfounded—you might be part of "Guess Culture" instead of "Ask Culture." Writer Andrea Donderi described these concepts on the blog MetaFilter.com back in 2007, and the post garnered a bit of viral attention because it resonated so strongly with readers. She wrote that people who are part of Guess Culture avoid asking for what they want unless they feel 100 percent positive that the answer will be an easy, breezy yes. The possibility of getting a no response is too

Dear Friendshipping,

After breaking up with my long-term partner, I am moving out of our shared house and into a new place by myself for the very first time. I'm excited, but it's also really daunting—all the packing and painting and moving. I confided these feelings to my mom, who told me this is the right time to ask friends to step up. She's probably right, but I'm worried that things like packing, painting, and moving are just too much to ask. What's the best way to ask for help that isn't too pushy?

Hold a "Help Me Move" event. Treat it like an open house. From 8:00 a.m. to 5:00 p.m., friends can come by whenever it is convenient for them to help! Get confirmations from people, and be understanding if they back out.

You could also send out a mass email asking for help throughout the week. As always, use the words that feel right for you, and BCC everyone. Include a description of the situation, what you need help with, what it would mean for you to be helped, and how you plan to thank your friends: "Hey all! I officially move into my own place at the end of the month. I'll be packing, moving, and painting every evening for the week of the twenty-fifth, and I could really use some help. If you've got a spare couple of hours to help me put things in boxes or take things out of boxes, please get in touch by responding to this email with which evening you can come by. Thank you so much, everyone!"

Finally, consider who specifically you might want help from. When Trin last moved, she knew that her friend Tomo was the only human strong enough to carry her hand-built wardrobe down two flights of stairs. Because she knew she needed this specific kind of help, she sent Tomo a personal request instead of the mass email. Thanks, Tomo!

uncomfortable, too awkward, too big of a risk, so Guessers rarely voice their asks. On the other hand, Askers have no trouble making requests. To them, the potential no is a harmless outcome.

Are you an Asker or a Guesser? Like so many midwesterners, we're Guessers. We live in terrible fear of inconveniencing people, especially when we're guests or patrons. If we were served the incorrect meal at a restaurant, we would rather chow down on the wrong food than inform our server of their mistake. Meanwhile, people who are part of Ask Culture would find this understandably ridiculous and ask for the correct meal without hesitation, no harm done. To be clear, there's not a correct side here—there are advantages and disadvantages to both Ask and Guess. Guessers often don't get what they need, like raises at work. Askers can come off as rude or demanding for simply being direct. Keep all this in mind when you need or request favors; your friend could be speaking from the opposite side of you.

IF YOU CAN HELP, SAY SO

Let's say that you're in a position to do favors. You're not experiencing emotional difficulty, but your friend is. In this case, you ought to *make it known* that you are available for favors. Saying, "Let me know if I can do anything to help" is vague, and then the burden is on the other person to come up with an answer. Be specific about what favors you can do. You cannot coach a friend through their long-term depression, but you *can* drop off fresh groceries. You can make sure their public transportation card is stocked with enough money so they can get to work on time in the morning. You can make sure their dishes are washed and their dog has been walked. When you reach out to help, make it as easy as possible for your friend to accept the favor. Do most of the legwork. Keep the offer short and uncomplicated, and try not to occupy too much of their time or brainspace:

- *Are you and the fam going to be home this evening? I am ordering pizzas to your door around 7:00 p.m. unless you tell me otherwise. Tip will be taken care of too.*
- *You've been taking the train to the hospital, right? I can drive you. I am available every evening this week. Just send me a text if you are up for it.*
- *If you want an afternoon to yourself, I would love to take the kids to the park on Saturday.*
- *If you are going to stay at your parents' for the rest of the month, I don't mind checking on your house. I can cut the grass and grab your mail.*
- *Do you have someone to take care of Lucky and Dave while you travel to the funeral? If not, I am happy to drop by and take care of them. If you leave me a key in the mailbox, I will make it happen.*

And in turn, if your friends are offering their help, try to let them, even if it makes you feel strange at first. You're allowed to share your burdens. In times of worry and doubt and sadness, friends can be true gifts.

FRIENDS AND FINANCES

WHEN YOU'RE ON A BUDGET

The amount of money you have should not matter at all in a friendship. But let's be realistic: If there's an imbalance, it can be difficult. Money is a major limiter on what you can do with a friend or a group of friends. If you're on a stricter budget than your pals and they're planning to go out for an expensive meal—yet again—consider doing this:

OFFER AN ALTERNATIVE AND TAKE ON THE WORK. "This restaurant isn't in my budget right now. Do you want to go to this place in particular, or do you mind if I find something else in the area that works better for me?" Or "Actually, I've already spent most of my eating out money for the month, but I would be up for something like [this less expensive place] or [this less expensive other place]."

MAKE IT CLEAR THAT MONEY IS IMPORTANT TO YOU. "I've got to stick to my budget, so I'm gonna skip this particular dinner. Have a great night, y'all."

GIVE A REASON—IF YOU WANT. "I'm saving for a massage chair, so I'm trying to cut back on eating out at restaurants." Or "I'm putting most of my money toward student loans right now, but keep me in the loop for future activities!"

These requests are completely reasonable, which means, in turn, any reasonable person will accept your spending limitations and not pressure you to attend or make you feel bad. In spite of this, if you find yourself feeling uneasy about bringing it up, use metathinking to examine your feelings and where they are coming from.

- *Am I being unkind or unfair to myself about this?*
- *Wouldn't I be understanding to someone on a budget if our roles were reversed?*
- *What can I do to feel better about this situation?*
- *Am I the first person ever in the world to be money conscious?*
- *Is it unreasonable or shameful to miss a dinner out?*

- *Am I supposed to feel bad about this? What's the evidence that I am supposed to feel bad about this?*
- *My friends and I just budget differently. Is there anything actually wrong with that?*

It might feel awkward and clumsy to speak up, especially if going out to eat is the norm for everyone else, but it gets easier with practice. (Plus, there could be other people in the friend group who feel the same way you do.) Remember that you're not wrong to ask for a simple change of plans. Likewise, your friend is not wrong for assuming you're A-OK with the way things are going if you've never spoken up before. You have to signal that you are making a change in where you want to eat, and you need to clue in your friend or group of friends. (It's also possible a

Dear Friendshipping,

My friend owes me $40. When I last mentioned it, he laughed. I've told him I'm serious but he doesn't seem to care. I'm afraid if I push the issue it'll create tension. On one hand, it's only $40. On the other hand, he borrowed it a year and a half ago and it still bugs me when I think of it. How do I bring this up?

This is a symptom of a broader issue: He is not listening to you, nor is he taking your needs into account. If he continues to laugh at you when you ask in person (ugh!), try sending a short email or text. "Hey, I need that $40 back. Could you bring it to lunch tomorrow?" And don't say anything else. Not "Sorry to ask again," or "I know it's not really a big deal." Hopefully if you put this in simple terms he can't argue with, it will resolve. If it doesn't, you may be out $40 (sorry about this), but you have learned important information about this particular friend and how he treats people—specifically, how he treats you.

friend will offer to cover your dinner costs. It's entirely your decision how to proceed there.) If your friends have lots of extra spending money, it can feel difficult to get them to be mindful of people who do not have similar means. But good food does not necessarily mean *expensive* food. If you enjoy eating it, then it *is* good food. Some of the most memorable and satisfying meals we've had in Chicago were pretty damn cheap. Potlucks, dive bars, delis, food trucks, late-night diners—these places are just as fun and worthy as those candlelit small bites spots.

Inexpensive & Free
THINGS TO DO WITH FRIENDS

- Laugh at your old yearbooks together
- Make something the long way, like bread, pie, or pizza
- Go for a hike
- Start a podcast
- Organize your closets and donate or swap clothes
- Have a potluck dinner
- Play poker, Frisbee, soccer, or catch
- Write a play or musical based on your friendship
- Have an at-home spa day
- Hold a video game tournament
- Go thrifting
- Design a board game, card game, puzzle, or scavenger hunt
- Have a talent show
- Design an art project— the uglier, the better
- Bring a bottle of wine to the park
- Create your own version of Pictionary, Scattergories, or charades
- Camp in your backyard
- Rearrange furniture
- Start a garden

But be prepared for this: Your friends, as wonderful as they are, will likely forget that you're on a budget. Adults are so bad at remembering details like these, unless those details make them feel some strong emotion (anger, shock, horniness). It's very possible that your friends will keep forgetting and keep inviting you to another expensive place that you have to turn down. They like your company, they want you there, and they probably aren't giving this much more thought than that; people who have disposable income are not always mindful of people who don't. We are sorry about this, but you will probably have to tell your friends multiple times that you are looking for inexpensive hangouts only, and you'll probably have to take on some of the work yourself in planning inexpensive outings. You can enlist a close friend in the group to help you with this, though. Explain your dilemma to a trusted pal in the group:

- *I could use some help reminding our friends that I'm not up for spending lots of money. Are you cool being my ally on this?*
- *Can you do me a favor? I feel like I am always the one suggesting we go somewhere less expensive. Next time that happens, can you help me find some alternate options to share with the group?*
- *Our friends forget that I'm on a budget. It's not their fault, everyone forgets stuff. But do you think you could add your voice to the convo during the planning stages?*
- *I won't be able to attend the more expensive outings for a while. If you could help me remind the group that some of us are more budget-conscious, that would be really helpful and put me at ease.*

If missing the expensive outings negatively impacts your friendships, that says way, way more about the friendships than about you. Money is not a demonstration of your worth as a friend or as a human being, and advocating for what you need does not make you the Great Ruiner of Fun.

LOANING MONEY TO FRIENDS: GOOD IDEA OR BAD IDEA?

Everybody has a different relationship with money. It's like the relationship you have with your parents: It's totally unique to you, it's complicated, it's personal, and it's kind of hard to explain to another person (at least without revealing a slew of private information). Amounts of money mean different things to different people. For some folks, picking up a pal's $5 bar tab doesn't even register as a purchase. For others, that $5 is essential—it might be budgeted specifically for their bus ride to work. So let's start with this basic tenet: It *is* OK to say no to a friend who asks to borrow money. You can also say yes! Before you say yes, though, make sure you are absolutely crystal clear on the expectations for both sides, since problems arise when we leave too much unspoken. You must be in total agreement on the definitions of the words "loan" and "borrow" because these words are thrown around loosely. Figure out whether your friend is asking for a loan that they will pay back or a gift that they will not. (This is why people make contracts or get things in writing—so there is no confusion later on.)

Let's say that your friend wants a loan, and they promise they will pay you back. You are entering an agreement of sorts, which is a complex layer to add atop a friendship. Before you loan the money, you should ask yourself these questions and come up with concrete answers:

- *When is the money due back to me? Am I comfortable setting a deadline from the outset?*

- *If they can't pay me back on time, how will that impact me financially? Emotionally?*
- *Am I going to feel comfortable holding my friend to this deadline?*
- *How am I going to ask my friend for the money if they miss the deadline? What would that convo look like?*

Depending on your answers, you might be the kind of person who can treat this like a business transaction, because it is. That doesn't mean you're cold, rude, or unfeeling—it means you're confident that you can be direct and upfront about what you need, and that you'll set expectations properly from the beginning, like so:

- *I can cover gas costs for our road trip. Let's just keep track of the receipts so you can pay me back by the end of the year. How's that sound?*
- *Happy to lend you the cash. Will you be able to pay me back by the end of the month?*
- *I can definitely loan you money for your airfare! When do you think you'll be able to pay me back? Let's set a date beforehand so this is stress-free for us.*
- *I can lend you that $200 you asked for. I just need it back by June 1.*

Give the gift of clarity and say what you need. But if you have any significant reservations, like you are feeling worried about your own financial situation or you're too uncomfortable having a conversation about repayment, it's best to say no. Do so quickly, concisely, and without much emotion in any direction—you don't want to make your friend feel embarrassed or ashamed for asking for help. Likewise, you do not

Dear Friendshipping,

My friend asked me if she could borrow some money to pay her rent next month. Is this a bad idea? I want to do it and I can afford it, but I'm worried about how this will impact our friendship.

We wish we could yell, "Of course! Loan the damn money!" But life is so much more difficult and unjust than that. You'll have to ask yourself some questions that might make you feel icky. Do you want a say in how she uses your money? Will you be mad if she doesn't use the money to pay her rent specifically? What if she uses it to pay off some of her debt? Or does it not really matter as long as she's OK, or as long as she pays you back? What are the best, worst, and most likely outcomes? What is her plan for paying you back, and are you 100 percent happy with this plan? Lending a friend money can be a tremendous kindness. We recommend doing it if, and only if, you feel at peace with the worst-case scenario, and won't suffer without the cash.

need to feel shame or embarrassment for being unable to or choosing not to provide the cash. Details and explanations are not necessary here; you don't need to reveal your financial history as proof. "I'm sorry, I can't lend money to anyone," or "It's just not in the budget right now," or "I'm sorry, I'm unable to cover this," are all impersonal, dispassionate responses. In this case, that's the right tone to strike so that it signals a courteous end to the conversation. If your friend presses for more information, you can repeat yourself, and do so without apology. Say something like, "Please don't put me in the position to have to say no twice," and that's that. Not "I'm sorry to be a jerk about this," or "I can try to adjust my budget." Hold firm to your response.

Even if you're a millionaire—in which case, please purchase dozens of copies of this book and give them away—that doesn't mean you've automatically opted in to giving away your money to whomever asks for it. Everyone has reason to keep close tabs on their money (saving for someone's education, donating to charity, helping a parent retire—anything someone deems a personal priority), and simply being the "rich friend" shouldn't broadcast to your friends that you're always available to offer a loan. That said, if your friend is financially hurting and you have the means, consider giving them the money with zero expectation that you will ever get it back. Land on an amount of money that you are comfortable with never seeing again. Maybe giving your friend the $50 they need for groceries this week could be an early and very useful birthday present.

Once you hand over the cash, though, you don't get to decide how the money is spent. Loaning a friend some money does not give you any say in their finances. This money is theirs now, and how and when it's used is no longer your business. That means you can't side-eye the decorative candles they put in their basket at Target. Don't

HITTING THE PAUSE BUTTON

What if your friend unexpectedly asks you for a loan? If you are put on the spot and feel rushed to give an answer, you can always defer. "Let me check on some things and get back to you" is a polite way to hit the pause button on the conversation. And then, of course, give them a solid yes or solid no at a later time, hopefully sooner rather than later. (By the way, the phrase "let me get back to you on that" works well in lots of situations, not just with loaning money. It allows you to gather your thoughts and metathink through what you feel.) This is an especially good practice for people who tend to say yes immediately or have trouble saying no. Add it to your vocab.

scowl at Instagram photos of them eating tacos at a restaurant instead of cooking at home. Unless your friend specifically asks you to bust open their financial records, it's not your place to give your opinion. You don't know their budget, the cost of their rent, their family history, medical records, health insurance plan, or who even paid for those tacos. Besides all that, you don't know what small joys help them get through the day. We live in an unequal and imperfect world, and we're doing our best. People are allowed to enjoy life and eat their damn tacos.

THE JOY AND STRESS OF GIVING GIFTS (AND WHY YOU DON'T HAVE TO DO IT)

You certainly don't *have* to give gifts to your friends, even for birthdays or holidays. There are dozens of ways to show love and support to your people, and giving presents does not have to be one of them. Do you lend a listening ear during rough times? Drive them to work when the weather is crappy? Attend their improv shows? (Sorry to hear that.) Those are gifts, too. You can be a thoughtful person even if you have never once bought a present. Besides, some of your friends probably hate physical gifts, and with good reason: They can inspire weird feelings! If we spend more on one friend than another, does that indicate that we like them better? If we spend too much, is that showing off? If we spend too little, does that mean we don't care? Money is so often a false signifier of care, competence, or social status. If we don't spend the "correct" amount, what are we saying? What is the "correct" amount? What does that even mean, and how can we find a balance?

Our first piece of advice: Give up on being perfect at this. Forget about "winning Christmas" or making your friend weep with joy when they open your gift. Your guilty feelings about gift-giving are largely influenced by capitalism and shame. Your worry and effort are probably the result of the corporate influence that entices you to buy things. So if you would like to quit doing gifts, that is a reasonable decision to make. Just tell your pal that you are making a change. A few examples:

- *Hey, is it cool if we skip presents this year? What if we get together and cook a meal instead?*
- *Are you still up for doing presents this year? If so, can we limit it to under $15? I'm on a budget.*
- *Idea: Let's skip presents this year and save ourselves time and money.*
- *An early heads-up: Presents are not in the budget for me this time around. I would love to just hang out and drink spiked hot chocolate with you.*
- *I would love to celebrate our birthdays this year by doing something together rather than exchanging gifts. For yours, want to grab a beer? Or see a movie?*
- *I'm buying gifts for my entire extended family this year, so is it OK if you and I skip presents?*

Alternatively, if gift-giving has never been part of your friendship but you'd like it to be, consider notifying your friend ahead of time so they aren't totally perplexed and stricken with guilt when you hand them a present. You don't need to tell them what it is, but you can offer "Hey, I know we don't usually do gifts, but I stumbled across the funniest thing for you that I had to grab. It's not a big deal." And don't expect anything in return. That is why it is called a "gift." Otherwise, it would be called a "trade." More tips for getting better at this:

START MAKING LISTS. We recommend making a chart or spreadsheet with at least two columns: one with your friends' names, the other with your gift ideas. This might seem like a lot of work, but it is so, so helpful. Next time you hear your friend say something like, "You know what I love more than my own children? Extra-dark chocolate," you have a place to save this nugget and you'll know precisely what to get them six months in the future.

Dear Friendshipping,

My oldest friend and I are in our late twenties and have been close since we were kids. She is really committed to elaborate and expensive birthday and Christmas presents. It's sweet, but I can't keep up or even afford it at this point. It's stressful! What are my options here?

Wouldn't it be great if gifts were just gifts? If we as a society never had to weigh the monetary value of a gift, or never felt any obligation to reciprocate? We don't live in that world, but still, you do have choices. You can say:

1. **"Let's not exchange presents."** How committed is this friend to giving presents, anyway? Well, you're about to find out. Still, this is a totally reasonable request even if they feel strongly.

2. **"Let's have a spending cap on presents."** Fair warning: This might turn into her making you something handmade and heartfelt, so if you're not at peace with that, go back to Option 1.

3. **"Let's do a completely different thing."** What if instead of a gift exchange, you go out for dessert? Or build a LEGO Death Star together? Or watch horny Netflix game shows and bake elaborate sugar cookies? Holidays and birthdays are meant to celebrate the joy of having each other in our lives, so you could just do that instead!

YOU CAN REGIFT. Regifting is good for the environment and good for your budget. Remember *Battlestar Galactica*? Of course you do, nerd. Admiral Adama loved his collection of books. He was on a spaceship far from home, so books were a commodity. Yet he freely gave away the ones he had already read—he knew that they would do more for someone who hadn't read them—rather than keep them sitting on his shelf as part of a collection, untouched. He never loaned them—he only gave them as gifts. Books work well for regifting because if they are a little worn and torn, that means that they were well-loved, and it's extra meaningful to receive something so personal. But anything else you regift (candles, booze, perfume, artwork) oughta be in basically pristine condition.

STOCKPILE SOME GIFTS. If your budget allows, keep scented candles or Starbucks gift cards nearby in case you're ever caught off guard by a kind gesture. While you're at it, having a package of blank greeting cards on hand is a good idea too.

STILL, REMEMBER THAT YOU AREN'T OBLIGATED TO GIVE GIFTS IN TURN. Listen, we'd all love to have the time, money, and energy to give thoughtful, heartfelt presents to everyone in our lives. But guess what: Not gonna happen. It's just not! If Jordan in Accounting bakes you holiday treats and you have nothing to give in return, you can simply say,

"Thank you for thinking of me, I love peppermint cookies," even if you don't love peppermint cookies. Spend twenty seconds thanking Jordan and lying if you have to. (It would be extra nice of you to also leave a personal note of thanks on Jordan's desk the next day.) **IF YOU CAN'T FIND THE PERFECT GIFT, YOU CAN ALWAYS DONATE TO A CHARITY IN YOUR FRIEND'S NAME.** Find an organization that aligns with your friend's values and hopes for the world and print out the donation certificate or use a blank card to write about your donation. (You don't even have to disclose the amount of money.) Every year, Jenn's friend group does this type of holiday gift exchange: They draw names at random and everyone makes a donation in their chosen friend's name. Friends have donated on Jenn's behalf to a Chicago animal shelter and an organization that serves marginalized groups of women. One year, Jenn was responsible for a friend whose biggest passion is biking. She did some research and found an organization that supports bicycle safety and laws. There are charities and orgs for everything! Warm fuzzies all around.

WORK, WORK, WORK, WORK, WORK FRIENDS

How and when you socialize at work impacts your workplace status. Our best tip comes from hormonal teenage Trin, who attended a Christian youth camp. Whenever Trin hung out with her male friends at camp, the counselors would warn, "Leave room for Jesus!" She was meant to believe that Jesus needed to be physically betwixt her and boys, involved in their every move. In situations where you'd like to be friends with your boss and coworkers, you unfortunately have to leave room for capitalism. You don't get to choose your colleagues like you do your friends, and power dynamics are always in play.

FRIENDING THE PERSON IN CHARGE

You should always let your boss think/believe that you are friends. That's just a savvy way to do business. But in reality, they will always be your boss first. You can be *friendly*, you can be friend-*like*, you can even be on excellent terms—but you cannot be true friends with the person who grips the reins of your employment, schedule, salary, and/ or benefits. If you're a boss yourself, you are not truly friends with your staff. Even if you're really fun and laid-back. Even if you work in one of those hip open offices where everybody sits on exercise balls. Above every other title, you are still the boss. Your staff never forgets this, and you shouldn't, either. That means when you ask an employee to attend an extracurricular work function (like a dinner, happy hour, or community service day), they'll feel obligated to accept the invitation. They'll probably even turn their schedules upside down to accommodate you. It's uncomfortable to say no to the person in charge! That's the real crux of the issue: Employees do not have the power to say no to the boss easily and comfortably. The element of honesty, too, is lost. Friendships rely on trust, and employees can't hold a 100 percent honest conversation with their boss without feeling like there might be career consequences, immediately or down the line. So be cautious! These power imbalances are a lot to overcome.

FINDING YOUR WORKPLACE FAVES

Many, many friendships are forged in the workplace. In fact, this is how your humble narrators met! Jenn and Trin worked together, bonded over a shared love of the video game *Mass Effect*, and became actual friends about ten minutes after that. There was an instant click. (This is a friendship phenomenon known as "getting lucky.")

Coworkers can quickly become friends because they spend so many of their waking hours at work. You can describe your workday

Dear Friendshipping,

I started a new job, and my new coworkers are attempting to befriend me. I'm not sure I want to be pals! Do I have to befriend coworkers? Should I be trying harder to make friends at work?

You don't have to be friends with anyone you don't want to. That's actually one of the best parts of adulthood; you can be selective about who you give your time to (for the most part, anyway). You should be selective.

You are a member of a workplace, however, and your behavior matters. So let's examine it. Who do you tend to give your time and attention to at work? Are you being respectful? Are you actively challenging your biases? What if you're only nice and patient to the people in charge?

Also, research shows you are more likely to be recognized, rewarded, and promoted if you participate socially at your job. So there are some advantages you might be missing out on. This isn't fair, of course. And this doesn't mean you have to start attending all the work happy hours, either! You can weigh the costs and benefits and still not attend a single happy hour; that's a decision you can make. We just want you to be able to make this choice with all the pros and cons in mind.

to your partner or vent about it to your mom, but your colleague knows exactly what happened for eight to twelve hours of your day—the good and the bad and everything in between. We recommend going out of your way to be kind and courteous to your coworkers. Beyond the potential networking benefits, it's great for your mental health to have a friend who enjoys seeing your face every day and vice versa. (Of course, while some coworkers are great, others are just awful. Then the best you can do is tolerate and/or avoid them.)

Work friends can make your job easier, in little and big ways; they can remind you about that deadline, cheer you on during a presentation, edit your work, or share their snacks. (Jenn and Trin once shared an office drawer filled with supplies, including emergency deodorant.) Work friends can even cover for you when you mess up. (To be clear, we mean in an "Oh, he was totally at the cash register on time, not ten minutes late!" type of way; we're not encouraging you to commit corporate fraud.)

Being friends with your coworkers also counts as networking. Sorry to say this, but the capitalist reality is that you're likely to see greater success in your field if you have a wide network of contacts you get along with. If you want to make friends at work but don't consider yourself particularly extroverted or social, be a slightly more helpful and outgoing version of your regular self. It's like acting in a play; there are some actions and scripts you can follow. Ask your coworkers if they want anything from the cafeteria since you're headed that way. Eat lunch with the group sometimes. Be the one who makes the coffee for everybody. Do the small-talk thing and ask what they did over the weekend, and be ready to give your own answer that is beyond "Oh, nothing, just hung out." If you're a new or recent hire, you can safely assume that no one besides the hiring manager remembers your name or anything about you. It's not your fault—people are distracted at work and not often in "meeting people" mode. Introduce yourself early and often. Trin once made friends at an old office job by waiting patiently in the break room with a work-appropriate board game and asking everyone who walked by if they wanted to play during lunch.

But workplace friendships do come with risks. We wish we could say that work means meeting all kinds of new friends! Every new hire is an opportunity for friendship! Hooray! But that's just not true. Your colleagues determine the mood of the workplace, where you will

presumably go most days until you change jobs, retire, or die. There's no easy escape from these people. These relationships could indirectly impact your wages, your position, and when you are scheduled to clock in for the day. That's why we recommend a warm-but-cautious approach when getting close to people at work. We want these friendships to be light and low-maintenance because if things go poorly, your job could be impacted. Here's what to keep in mind when you're befriending colleagues:

YOU MIGHT NOT LIKE EVERYTHING YOU FIND. Once you get to know people as friends, you may learn something unpleasant—their politics, what horrors live in their internet browser history—and you can't just delete that from your memory or completely disengage. When you have to work closely with that coworker, you will still know that they are the type of person who throws garbage out the windows of their car or thinks women suck at sports. You're stuck with them, basically.

FRIENDS FIGHT. Friends disagree and argue. Friendships end, some-times badly. Can you keep this out of the workplace? Do you want the added stress of keeping a lid on your emotions? Disagreements with coworkers have more serious consequences than disagreements with other friends.

GOSSIP IS A LEGITIMATE CONCERN. This is a pessimistic viewpoint, but assume that any secret you share with one coworker will reach every other person within a half-mile radius by, say, lunchtime. Pretend any email you send from your work address will be shared with your boss, *their* boss, the human resources department, your cubicle buddy, your grandmother, or appear on the front page of the *New York Times* tomorrow. This probably won't happen. But it could, and you gotta look out for yourself. You want the spotlight on you for positive reasons only. People with boring jobs are especially craving entertainment. You don't want to be the entertainment.

THERE'S ALWAYS A HIERARCHY. Your friend could become your boss, or you could become *their* boss, and you shouldn't pursue a close per-sonal relationship (friendly or romantic) with anyone who works under you in the company structure. What if you get a promotion, and your friend doesn't, and they're sad and jealous? What if your friend is put in charge of an exciting project that you really thought you deserved? It would be awesome if everyone could push this kind of thing aside in the name of friendship, but that's not easy to do when your health insurance / rent / future is on the line. It takes special chemistry to overcome a competitive workplace. It can certainly be done, but it's a tough ask for some people.

We're giving you these warnings to prevent conflict and hardship down the line, but we still recommend participating in work socializa-tion, if and when you can. There are so many legitimate reasons why this is difficult to accomplish. Maybe you have mobility concerns. Or you're over a decade older than everyone in your department. Or you can't go to Jason's for a cold brewski because you need to get home to tuck your twins into bed. Maybe you're just shy, tired after work, or hate your boss. But when you *can* take an hour or a few to hang with your coworkers (especially when your direct manager will be there), you might want to super consider doing it. It shows you care about your job (even if you don't) and that you gel with your colleagues. It's an opportunity to show your awesome personality. If you work in a huge company, your presence might simply remind your boss that you exist. So when the stars magically align and you have nothing else planned, go to the happy hour, the mini-golf outing, whatever fun thing is planned. Remember:

YOU DON'T HAVE TO STAY LONG. If you're not feeling it, show your face, have a few conversations, and make your graceful exit. Then you can return home, secure in the knowledge that you made an effort to maintain functioning relationships with your coworkers.

COMPLAIN RESPONSIBLY. Fact: When colleagues get together, they will complain. It just happens, especially if alcohol is flowing. It's how coworkers bond. You can enjoy tremendous relief while unloading with folks who completely understand your shared work life, but do stay mindful. Know who you are speaking to and what will undoubtedly be repeated later on. Keep your wits about you.

REMAIN MOSTLY PROFESSIONAL. Even if you're at a bar and not technically at work anymore, pretend that you are. Know your limits with alcohol / weed / any other substance. And if you don't know your limits, don't partake until you do. A work event is not the place to start experimenting. You have to act professionally enough that the human resources director isn't waiting at your desk in the morning. Being professional means you are not being your fullest, funniest, weirdest self. You aren't acting the same way as you would around your regular friends, because most real friendships are decidedly not professional. You can drunk-text your friends at 3:00 a.m. Not the case here.

Surface-level conversations are well-suited for this setting:

- *It's so [sunny / cold / windy / hot] outside! I [hate / love / tolerate] this weather. How about you?*
- *How long have you worked [in this department / at this company / in this industry]?*
- *What brought you to [this department / this company / this industry]?*
- *I love the photos of sunsets that you keep on your desk! Did you take those yourself?* (A general rule: If you see something nice, say something nice. If you notice something interesting out in the open—so, not a website that was open on someone's laptop, not something inside their desk drawer, not something inside their locker, but rather, framed pictures of kids on their desk, a novel on their bookshelf, a plant in the window—you can say something nice about it. Everybody loves to hear how adorable their kids, pets, and plants are or that they have great taste in art and books.)

Don't ask these types of questions, which will get your ass kicked and/or fired:

- *When do you plan on having (more) kids?*
- *Why are you taking medical leave?*
- *Who did you vote for? / Who are you going to vote for?*
- *Doesn't this [music / punch / pizza / corporate entity] suck?*
- *Why aren't you drinking? / Why are you drinking?*

LEVELING UP

You don't have to be buddies with all of your coworkers (or any of them), but you do have to show them basic respect. Try to remember their names and definitely learn their pronouns. From there, your relationships with colleagues can evolve and grow, like this:

COWORKER: You wish them well from afar. You have no particular interest in knowing more about them other than the basics. You probably would not be able to describe anything about them except "They seem nice!"

RESPECTED COLLEAGUE: You truly enjoy working with them. Their presence makes being at work easier on you. Perhaps you share a carpool, eat lunch together, or give each other birthday cards.

BOON COMPANION: You attend and enjoy social events together, like after-work happy hour. You have their phone number. You've grumbled about your boss together. You know their dog's name.

COMRADE-IN-ARMS: You know their dog's preferred brand of kibble because you've pet-sat for them. They follow you on your private social media accounts. You talk often outside of work. You share ideas, you gripe together, and you feel confident that the stuff you tell each other won't spread around the office.

FOR-REAL FRIENDS: You hang out outside of work often, you trust them, you've been through some shit together and you've come out on the other side. This is the kind of friendship that started at work, but it extends far outside the workplace. If one of you left the job, you'd still see them often.

MIXING BUSINESS AND FRIENDSHIP

When you go into business or collaborate on a project with a pal, you're adding another ingredient to your friendshipy stew. Before, your stew was made of beef cubes (shared history), carrots (humor), and potatoes (mutual friends). Now you're throwing in something new, like an entire stick of butter or a dainty squeeze of lemon. Sometimes the new ingredient will ruin the dish. Sometimes it completes the meal and you can't believe you ever made it another way.

Going into business or working on a project together is one of the rockiest roads you can take in a friendship. Some people say never, ever to do it because only ashes and rubble will remain once the friendship inevitably explodes and burns to the ground. That's fair! That's wise! Not working with friends is a reasonable policy to hold; you will save yourself stress in a world that is already so stressful, and you preserve the friendship. But some partnerships (like ours!) are not only doable,

Dear Friendshipping,

I've been working on a children's book, and I want to enlist my artist friend to help me illustrate it. What's the best way to approach this?

Are you trying to enlist your friend, or are you trying to *hire* them? Important difference here! Know exactly what you are asking, and make your goal clear. What kind of commitment are you looking for? Are you a professional asking for collaboration on a project that you want to pitch to publishers? Or do you see this as a fun extracurricular project with a buddy?

It's true that some people will volunteer or collaborate for free, but don't assume as much—assume your friend needs to be paid. Artists tend to be undervalued for their work, so you need to research the standard hourly rate for their specialty and tell your friend the deadlines you will ask them to meet, the scope of the work, the expected page count, and what kind of payment you can offer. Strike a tone that feels right for you; we suggest a mix of warmth, professionalism, and enthusiasm (you want to work with them for a reason, after all!). And of course, give your friend space and understanding if they don't accept.

but lead to incredibly rewarding work that could not be accomplished alone. We were coworkers for years before we started our podcast. We've sold stuff online, we managed a Kickstarter project, we partnered on this book. None of this was *easy,* of course, and it's not like we were smiling 100 percent of the time. We have felt unenthused, we have procrastinated, we have given each other pep talks to get things done, all of it. But our particular blend of chemistry and personalities just works, and we're honestly not sure why. It's likely because we share the same core life values. We're also completely honest about our strengths and expectations. We know our best skills and what we are laughably terrible at doing. That is why we hired a designer to do our visual design work and a producer to edit our podcast. We agreed that the time we gained from the skilled labor was worth the cost of hiring someone, thus we receive very little profit from our "business." To us, the creative endeavor has always been the main priority, because we agreed that we would rely on our full-time jobs for the bills. Without this understanding, one of us could have been very disappointed.

So if you're thinking about teaming up with a friend as we have, here is what to assess, on your own or together:

EMOTIONAL RISK. Are you confident that your friendship can withstand disagreements? How will your disagreements impact your relationship with mutual friends? Are you in a place where you can bring additional stress into your life?

RESOURCE RISK. Money is important, obviously, but so is your time. How many hours a day will you be investing? How about your friend? Is it possible to work together on a smaller project that has a set end date first, rather than overcommitting? Lay out how many hours of your week you're willing to dedicate to this project. How flexible is your Tuesday night brainstorm session?

PUBLIC RISK. And in case things don't work out, what happens? What does failure look like to both of you? If it's a low-risk project, perhaps very little would change about your lives. But if it's a huge and public undertaking, make sure you share the same feelings about public failure, loss of network, and loss of standing/respect in your industry.

If you both feel comfortable with those risks, there are also a few things you and your friend need to decide (to the best of your capabilities) before you hold hands and leap into these murky waters:

WHO DOES WHAT. You need to assign responsibilities, both right now and in the hypothetical foggy future. If something goes wrong, who will handle it? If this is a shared investment, who takes the hit? Don't pretend that the tasks will be magically divided up—make sure that every single (foreseeable) task is assigned.

HOW FEEDBACK IS DELIVERED. Giving feedback is a skill. Receiving feedback is a skill, too! Are you comfortable sharing your profesh criticisms with your friend? In the early days of our podcast, for example, Trin taught Jenn how to hold a microphone without breathing heavily into it. Her feedback was painless, helpful, warm, and funny; no harm done. We always recommend using the Feedback Scale: "What level of feedback are you looking for, on a scale of one to ten?" A one means "mostly praise, encouragement, and minor grammatical corrections." A ten is "set every sentence ablaze and let a new draft rise from the ashes."

HOW DECISIONS ARE MADE. Does your friend need approval from you before they make a business decision? Who gets the final say? Do you need an update every time they, say, use their company card to get coffee? Figure out which decisions can be made solo and which ones need consensus.

HOW TO DISAGREE SENSIBLY. Look back on your history together. Have you ever had and resolved a disagreement with your friend? What is their fighting style? Can they be reasoned with once they're emotionally or financially invested in an outcome? Disagreements are inevitable, so you need to know if you can work through them as a team.

YOUR PRINCIPLES AND VALUES. A certain amount of disagreement is productive—you want a partner who challenges your thinking and widens your perspective. Even if you don't share their point of view, you should at least *respect* it. . . . Unless you can't. If one of you wants to invest in green energy and the other wants to hide your profits in offshore accounts, you don't share the same vision. If one of you wants to give your device to Doctors Without Borders and the other wants to sell it to the military, you may want to rethink your match. It could be far less obvious: Maybe one of you wants to build up a nest egg, and the other wants to spend cash to grow quickly. These are conversations to have early on in order to avoid unpleasant surprises down the line.

THE EVERYDAY STRESSES. If you're on a deadline and you know that your friend is playing video games instead of working, are you gonna lose your shit? If your friend hasn't answered your time-sensitive email, what then? Are you going to call their cell? What if you know that they're at their kid's piano recital? You gotta be emotionally prepared for these moments.

Before you formally go into business or start a project with a friend—the kind that involves contracts, agreements, lawyers, or money—we believe that you gotta work on (and finish!) *at least* one project together. The project should have a deadline and apply pressure to both of you to participate—a project that you both are invested in completing. A fantasy football draft doesn't count. Creating one funny four-minute YouTube video doesn't cut it. You need to collab in a way that reveals how you both handle stress and organization, how long you take to reply to emails, the hours you prefer working (are you bursting with creativity at 7:00 a.m or at 2:00 a.m.?), how you cope with failure and embarrassment, how you celebrate success (as well as your definition of success versus their definition), and a million little things that don't matter in a friendship before this moment.

In the end, it's a risk, but some risks are worth taking. Nothing ventured, nothing gained, right? Isn't that how the saying goes? This could be the partnership you've always dreamed of. And we can't forget to mention this simple truth: Friends often have great ideas, and making things together is *fun*.

ENOUGH ABOUT BUSINESS: LET'S TALK ROMANCE

WHEN YOU HAVE A CRUSH ON A FRIEND

Crushes are so fun! So exciting! What a rush to experience the temporary psychosis of human attraction! If you are the type of person who gets romantic and/or sexual crushes, you will likely have a crush on one of your friends at some point. This is a very common and often temporary phenomenon that occurs because:

YOU ALREADY LIKE THEM AND HAVE INTERESTS AND HOBBIES IN COMMON. You're friends for a reason, after all. You already enjoy spending time together.

THEY'RE KIND TO YOU. In a dark world, it feels incredible to be loved and cared for.

THEY'RE NEARBY. Convenience is so alluring. That's why so many people hook up with their coworkers—they're right there.

YOUR FRIENDS ARE HOT. Look around you. They are.

Now that you're all excited, allow us to crush your spirit. First, take a giant, metaphorical step backward from this. You've got work to do! You need perspective, and you gotta assess your feelings thoroughly before sharing them aloud. We know this sounds neither fun nor sexy, but neither is most of adulthood.

Know this: If you tell your friend you have romantic feelings for them, their perception of you will change immediately and permanently, for better or for worse. They will never unknow that you have a crush. You can't hit a button that says UNDO, REDO, or SHAZAM! If you were to make your feelings known, you would be attempting to take

you and your friend into new territory, and they may not want to go with you. You could potentially upheave your entire friendship. And since crushes pass and fade, we want you to sit patiently with your feelings before acting on them. Enjoy your crush as you would, say, a delicious piece of fan fiction or dark chocolate cake.

After you've thought about it carefully, you might decide to keep your feelings to yourself. If so, consider taking a little time away from your friend. It doesn't have to be a big deal and doesn't require a major announcement. But quietly putting more stretches of time between your hangouts may help you feel good about your decision. Keep yourself busy with other friends and hobbies.

On the other hand, maybe you've thought about it and decided it is indeed time to admit your feelings. First, know that this will be a fraught and delicate conversation. Set up a time to talk in a setting that's neutral for both of you—somewhere you both have the ability to leave. (Imagine if you wanted to end this difficult conversation but your friend is still in your living room, or sitting next to you on the

Dear Friendshipping,

Lately I have been experiencing romantic feelings for a close friend and I am considering pursuing them. I'm getting pretty clear vibes that they like *me* like *me but I don't know if it's a good idea to disrupt our dynamic. How can I bring this up? Should I? How do I know when it's time?*

First, ask yourself if it would be all that bad to keep this crush to yourself just a bit longer. Consider it a test: What would that feel like? If this scenario is torturous to imagine, that's probably a sign that you should indeed share your feelings!

Also, do a little recon. If you've got mutual friends you trust, ask for their opinions. Are they noticing the same vibes you're picking up? Do they think you'd be adorable together?

Finally, as for the big reveal: Make it private, personal, and low pressure. Ask questions and encourage them to talk about their feelings. Be accepting if this doesn't go as planned, and be ready to wind down the conversation amicably.

train, trapped for the rest of the ride. Yikes.) Treat this like a breakup, because it potentially is one. *Don't blurt out your sexy thoughts one day because you just can't take it anymore.* Take a deep breath and a cold shower. You are not going to explode.

Clear communication is the right path here (and always), so don't cushion your words or nest them inside your beautiful, sweet poetry. That means you aren't sighing, "I've loved you ever since that day in gym class," or "You are the sole treasure of my beating heart." (You might do this anyway, but at least try not to.) Say something like "I've asked you here because I [am experiencing warm squishy feelings / am totally crushing on you / am interested in banging / like you as more than a friend]. I understand that I'm putting a lot on the line here."

"But I [think you might feel the same way / want to know what you think] and I believe that this is worth figuring out together."

Once you share your feelings, your crush might:

- Need space or distance from you
- Immediately respond that they like you, too
- Need some time to think
- Be shocked
- Be totally unsurprised
- Make you feel sad, confused, or embarrassed
- Question your motivations (they might think your friendship was just a ruse to try to become romantic and/or sexual with them)
- Launch themselves into your loving arms

Good or bad, there are always consequences to sharing your feelings aloud, and we want you to be prepared for the aftermath. In case you need 'em, here are some scripts for you to make a pleasant-enough escape:

- *I'm going to go into the other room and get a glass of water. And when I come back, let's act like this never happened. Sound good?*
- *Thanks for your honesty. Let's give each other space to absorb all of this.*
- *I'm going to take a walk to clear my head. I want this to be a blip in our friendship history. Could you text me when you feel ready to move on from this?*

Now let's explore the other possibility: that your crush likes you back. Aw! First of all, enjoy this moment—it's a special one. Then, know that you are transitioning into a new kind of relationship. Things are changing! To manage this change, it's important to:

LEAVE NO SUBTEXT. We get that no one wants to have the "so where is this going?" conversation right away. But if you have expectations regarding monogamy or fidelity, it's responsible to make those expectations clear as soon as it's comfortable.

REMEMBER THAT RELATIONSHIPS LOOK DIFFERENT ON EVERYONE. You don't have to follow any romantic platitudes that don't suit you. For example, there's this wacky myth going around that the gold standard of romance is marrying your "best friend." It may seem like everyone's marrying their best friend these days because a) "I married my best friend" sounds really lovely, so people like to say it, even if they have best friends other than their spouse, and b) the term "best friend" has no strict definition.

KNOW YOU WILL NEVER RETURN TO THE PREDATING STATE. Whether you break up or stay together forever or end up somewhere in between, there's no switch you can flip to start over. Lots of people stay friends after breaking up, of course. But there's no way to undate this person. You can't unknow what it was/is like to date them.

One last note here: If you share your feelings and then your crush says something like "in another world . . ." or "in another life . . ." or "if only I'd met you first, then we could be together" or "please wait for me," uh, you probably know that we're going to tell you to move the fuck on. Their feelings toward you depend on living in an alternate universe that does not exist. They would like you to remain stalled in their garage until they're ready to take you out for a spin. You deserve someone who is as enthusiastic about you as you are about them.

171

WHEN YOUR FRIEND HAS A CRUSH ON YOU

In the opposite situation, what if you think that your friend has a crush on you and the situation is not exactly fraught, but it is [awkward / confusing / inconvenient / embarrassing]? It *is* possible that your friend is only flirting because it's fun, not because they're nurturing feelings toward you. But if they are crushing and you don't feel the same, politely ignoring the crush is a viable option. Put some courteous distance between you and this crush-haver. Only hang out with them when you're in a group of people, for example. The group can act as a social buffer. You can enlist a trusted friend to discreetly help you with this. You could also simply not see them for a few weeks or months—it's OK to take breaks from people! It is possible to feel quietly flattered (crushes are flattering!) without letting your whole world go sideways. Continue to be your cool, level-headed self, remain comfortable in your friendship, and let time do its thing. Proceed a little more carefully, act sensitively to the crush-haver's feelings for you, and don't over-promise your time or attention.

Meanwhile, their feelings will probably burn off eventually. Most crushes are delicate spring roses that bloom, wilt, and die, and then are never plucked from the garden. For every sad, sighing tale that wonders, "What could have been?" there are thousands more

people thinking, "Whew, thank god we stayed just friends, because a relationship never, ever would have worked."

But what if it's not that easy? What if all of this is making you seriously uncomfortable? What if you have concerns about what will happen next? Maybe you are worried that your friend will try to kiss you, or you're feeling uneasy about how their behavior has changed. If anything like this rings true, listen to your emotions here. If you're being pursued or flirted with and you do not like it, that is absolutely worth speaking up about. Even if it's a friend. *Especially* if it's a friend. The title of "friend" is not a license to do whatever they wish without conse-

quence. Friends—even good friends and best friends—are capable of violating your consent in big and small ways. (And statistically, predators are not strangers; they are people you already know.) It is not selfish to take care of yourself. This will feel difficult and cost you emotional energy, but we recommend being as direct as you can about what you need. You can drop hints, you can be subtle, you can attempt to spare this person embarrassment, but what you are requesting, after all, is to be treated well. That's it. Not a lot to ask. If you were making a friend uneasy with your jokes or your physical contact, wouldn't you want to know so you could immediately self-correct?

When you are stating your boundaries, you do not need to be the most eloquent, sensitive, glowing person imaginable. You can do this imperfectly, feel flustered, stumble over your words—you still deserve to be heard. You do not need to become The Politest Person to Ever Live with a slew of polished and well-prepared explanations. When it comes to your personal safety, *you can be downright impolite.* As Oprah says, "The word 'no' is a complete sentence." Listen to Oprah on this one.

Make sure to list what specific behaviors need to change. Leave nothing up to their unreliable interpretation. Here are some scripts we have in mind for you:

- *Hey, I need you to know that I'm not cool with [hugs / you putting your hands on my waist / cuddling during the movies].*
- *You might not even realize you're doing it, but can you not do the surprise-shoulder-massage thing?*
- *When you call me "babe," it makes me feel weird. Can you knock that off? Please and thank you.*
- *Hey, this is the second time I've had to tell you I'm not comfortable with you surprise hugging me. Please don't.*
- *I need you to not show up to my office unannounced anymore. It puts me in an uncomfortable position at work.*
- *Those comments you leave on my Instagram photos are creepy. You gotta cut that out.*

How they respond to this will tell you their views on consent, respect, power dynamics, and you. Your request is not extreme, nor is it irrational. Your friend has the opportunity to make you feel a little safer and happier in the world. Friends should never make you feel uncomfortable on purpose. Even if they are the touchy-feely type. Even if you've known them since you were a kid. Even if they're well liked and otherwise nice; even if they regularly buy you dinner and pay for your movie tickets; even if they are going through a rough time in their life. Doesn't matter. Someone who disregards how they make you feel is not a friend. (More on that on page 195.)

A TALE AS OLD AS TIME: YOU DON'T LIKE WHO YOUR FRIEND IS DATING

Some of your friends will date dingdongs. Just total duds. This is a simple fact of life, so if nothing else, perhaps you can draw comfort from the fact that this is neither a new nor an uncommon problem. (To be

Dear Friendshipping,

I think a new-ish friend in our social circle has a crush on me. I'm totally flattered, but am not interested and don't want her to feel awkward. How do I navigate this without making her think I like her back?

If you can't determine a clear action to take, that might be a sign you don't need to take action yet! Or at all. It's very possible your friend will never bring this up herself, and the crush will just pass on its own, as crushes so often do. But if she does bring it up, tell her what you just wrote to us, because it's both honest and mature: Say that you're totally flattered by her feelings, but you're not interested in her that way, and you don't want her to feel awkward. Treat her as you would want to be treated if the roles were reversed.

clear, we are not referring to abusive relationships. If you suspect abuse is involved, please find a trusted and trained resource, like a treatment center or a hotline, to determine what steps you should take.)

But of course, there are always more unexceptional cases. In those situations, should you share your negative opinions with your friend? Maybe. Possibly. Probably not. Deliberate on these questions first:

WHEN YOU THINK YOUR FRIEND COULD "DO BETTER," WHAT DO YOU MEAN? Are you referring to their partner's looks? Their taste in music? Their career? Be brutally honest with yourself. Are your concerns superficial? Remember that your friend has different tastes and values, and they're allowed to make choices you disagree with. Keep yourself in check, too: For example, if you're all concerned because your friend is dating, say, a gas station attendant—that's not cool of you; don't be classist.

IS THIS JUST A MATTER OF PERSPECTIVE? Try to look at this from the viewpoint of your friend. Presumably they like their partner, so imagine what they see in them that you do not. Maybe they strike you as stand-offish or arrogant. But they might make your friend laugh all the time, be an excellent dinner companion, or have a dozen other attributes you don't see. List their possible awesome qualities, even if you have to guess what they are. Perhaps the sex is incredible! If nothing else, assume that your friend is having amazing sex.

HOW WELL DO YOU KNOW THIS PERSON? Truly calculate how much time you have spent in their company. Context and setting matter, too. Maybe they strike you as aloof or awkward because you only see them for five seconds before they disappear into your roommate's bedroom and shut the door. Conversely, maybe you spend way, way too much time around this person because you're often the third wheel on dates, or they're at your house so often that they're basically an additional room-mate (one who doesn't pay rent). None of these scenarios sets you up well for understanding and having patience with another person!

We want you to get to the heart of why you dislike them, because what matters most, of course, is how they treat others, and more specifically, how they treat your friend. So if you simply find them irri-tating, but they are generally courteous and seem to make your pal happy, you oughta keep your opinions to yourself. (But you can still limit your time with them. No need to devote hours to making yourself like someone you'll never mesh with.) Another option: Gather more

Dear Friendshipping,

My roommate is in a long-distance relationship, and it's so clearly making him miserable and lonely. He should be out living his life, not staying home, waiting around for a phone call. It's pretty obvi-ous they will be long distance for the next four years, and I don't know how to handle seeing my friend anxious, stressed, and alone. Can I say something?

Your friend is sad, and you don't want to add to his sadness. If the relationship becomes too difficult to maintain long distance, they'll break up on their own. And if they make it the next four years, good for them, right? Loads of people make long distance work! That said, if you feel like your friend would truly benefit from hearing from you, approach gently and with compassion: "I don't think that this situation is making you happy. I'm worried about you." Or "A clean break might be what is best for you both. Have you ever thought about that?" Once you've said your piece, that's it! He knows your opinion, and he gets to do what he wants with it.

information. Don't understand how your friend could date such a dingus? Ask! But avoid questions like this:

- *How can you date such a dingus?*
- *What do you even see in them?*
- *Are they ever going to be able to take you to a nicer restaurant?*
- *Why are you guys [moving so slow / moving so quickly / not moving forward]?*
- *So how come Joey never talks?*
- *So did Bessie finally get a job yet or what?*

Asking your friend to defend their partner when you don't know their partner very well is unfair of you. These conversation starters will prrrrobably go over better:

- *How's it going between you?*
- *How long have you been together now?*
- *How was your night out? Did you have a fun date?*
- *Are you getting serious, or is it more casual right now?*
- *Pacey seems shy and quiet—am I right about that?*
- *How's their job search going?*
- *I'd like to get to know Dawson better. Maybe we could all hang out sometime? What do you think?*

If you get in the habit of asking questions like these, you'll learn how the relationship is unfolding overall, and the blurry picture will become clearer to you. Everybody has bad days or off days with their partners. It's a series of bad days that should make your ears perk up. If you gather new information that seems to confirm that the relationship is indeed unfolding poorly, you can say what you're hearing, seeing, and noticing. After all, you are not an automaton. You are allowed to have opinions and judgments, especially regarding people who bum out your friends. Just make it clear that you are coming from a place of concern, not outright dislike (yet). Establish that you are on your friend's team. Like this:

- *If you're happy, I'm happy. But right now you do not seem happy.*
- *It's hard for me to see you like this.*
- *It does bother me when they say they will call you and then they don't.*
- *I think your partner owes you an apology on this one.*
- *This strikes me as an unfair situation to put you in!*
- *Can I ask you about Andie? Something they said at dinner tonight rubbed me the wrong way, and I want your take on it.*
- *It does worry me that they might be taking advantage of your generosity.*
- *I'm sensitive to the fact that you are [paying their rent / taking on all this work] for them.*

After broaching some of these questions, you might still be searching for an explanation. Unfortunately, that means you might be in the toughest situation of all: What if your friend does seem happy, but their partner still sucks? They are unkind, insensitive, disagreeable, and yet, for reasons beyond comprehension, your friend fails to see their flaws and adores their company. Then you have a decision to make: Do you want to stay close with someone who enjoys spending time with (in your opinion) an actual jerk? After all, you are the company you keep. Only you know the answer, but remember: Sometimes your friends will date and/or marry duds. This is one of life's greatest mysteries. You don't have to make yourself become friends with this person, and you don't even have to like them.

Should you say something to your friend, though? Well, first, imagine what your friend will say in response. Imagine their reaction. Will they be surprised or unsurprised that you have opinions on who they're dating? In other words, is this tricky topic one that you have broached successfully before? (And if the roles were reversed, would you hear out *their* thoughts?) "It's nothing against you, but I just don't like your boyfriend," is a difficult conversation to have, and we don't recommend it unless you feel you must. It's risky, but then again, the risk might be worth taking if you truly believe you can prevent your friend from experiencing excessive hardship, heartache, or financial ruin. But before you say a word, sincerely ask yourself, "How will sharing this information help my friend?" and make sure you have an answer.

CAN DUDES AND LADIES EVER BE JUST FRIENDS? AN INVESTIGATION

This question comes up a lot. Lucky for us, we both have soft ergonomic keyboards, so whenever we're asked this, we can safely bang our heads against our desks.

But honest inquiries deserve honest answers, so let's first examine the heteronormativity baked into this question, because it's an inaccurate profile of humanity. Heteronormativity is the assumption that all men are only attracted to women, and all women are only attracted to men. This also promotes the stereotype that men everywhere can't curb their sexual feelings. Obviously these things are untrue, so when you ponder if men and women can ever be "just friends," you are not only ignoring the existence of platonic friendship, you are also ignoring (or purposefully dismissing) the existence of people who are asexual

and/or not straight. Pretty unfortunate oversights there! Are gay men not allowed to be friends with other men? Are you saying that bisexual or pansexual people can't have any friends? Be truthful with yourself—you are not asking "can dudes and ladies be friends?" You're secretly wondering something like this:

- *Should I let my partner be around people they could find attractive?*
- *Should I be worried that my girlfriend has male friends?*
- *If I allow my partner to hang out with whomever they want, will they cheat on me?*

So, yes, you should "allow" your partner to hang out with whomever they wish, but with the understanding that healthy relationships do not include micromanaging. If you are constantly anxious about who your partner spends time with, that's a problem to address with your partner. You are coming from a place of insecurity—so many people feel

Dear Friendshipping,

Is it weird that my boyfriend's best friend is an attractive woman? It never bothered me until a friend pointed it out and said she "would NEVER be OK with that." I'm starting to feel weird by the implication here. Am I setting myself up to get cheated on?

You deserve a partner who is head over heels for you. Are there indications that this is not the case (other than the fact that your partner simply has a friend who is attractive)? Does he make you a priority? Do you feel good about your relationship? If not, then those are the problems that need to be addressed, and they aren't related to his attractive best friend.

But if the only issue is this attractive friend, and you still can't help but feel weird, that's also solvable. It could be that your own friend made this comment because she loves you, sees something you don't, and wants to protect you. But more likely, your friend is being kinda silly, because attractive people are everywhere. And sometimes they are our friends! Would you smooch every attractive person in your life? Probably not, and your boyfriend probably wouldn't, either.

This might not really be about the attractive best friend at all. Sometimes we just need extra confirmation that we are loved and cared for. Perhaps you want to say, "I know you love me, but it would mean a lot to hear it out loud a few extra times today." Or simply: "I'm feeling crappy. Can I have a compliment, please?"

insecure!—but maintaining a guest list for your partner is abusive and manipulative. Manage this problem with the help of someone who will be completely honest with you, like a therapist. You are not doomed, you are never beyond repair, but you do have homework: You have to begin changing your habits and the way you think.

By the way, it's also an ineffective means of curbing cheating. We have no idea if your partner is going to cheat on you. But if someone wants to cheat, they'll find a person to cheat with. Human beings live everywhere on this planet, even the very cold parts. Any determined party can and will find a human to kiss if given enough time and resources. People who cheat usually cheat with someone who's just, like, around. If it's not the attractive friend or that cutie from the office, it's someone else. But please don't take away from this that your partner wants to bang everyone who ends up "being around." That's not true. We're saying that if your partner cheats, for whatever reason they have for cheating, they'll probably end up picking from the pool of people near them. If you force a manipulative situation in which they do not have many people near them, they'll just look farther for a different person.

Back to the question: Can straight men and straight women ever remain "just friends"? Yes. They can. Of course they can. Whenever we're asked this, we worry that you believe platonic relationships will inevitably a) grow rotten, or b) ripen into sex or romance. Friendship is not simply sexual opportunity. This is why the idea of a "friend zone" is so troubling. Friendship is not romance in disguise, nor is it an inconvenience you must endure to get laid. Love and friendship can overlap, of course. Friendship can ease into romance. If you've been to lots of weddings, you've seen a version of this scene: The betrothed hold hands at the altar and say something like, "I can't believe I get to marry my best friend." Very sweet. But you do not need to marry your best friend if it doesn't work out that way, and it's not a goal to aspire to. If you choose to get married, marry a person who understands you deeply, and if they also happen to occupy the role of best friend, or were your friend first, that's cool. But friendship with the gender you're attracted to is not a stopgap. Friendships are worth cherishing as they are. Platonic love is not second best.

WHEN FRIENDSHIP GETS COMPLICATED

HOW TO FEEL BETTER ABOUT STANDING UP FOR YOURSELF (YOU CAN DO IT!)

Trin was once part of a very intense conference call with two very intense businessmen. A significant financial decision was up in the air. The men were on opposite sides, fighting like hell to get what they wanted. There was swearing and dick swinging, and it lasted over an hour. Finally, one man wore the other down and emerged victorious. Trin was both awed and horrified when she later asked him how he pulled it off and he said simply, "I knew I was correct."

Lesson learned: It's easier to advocate for yourself if you believe you are right. You shouldn't ever wear a friend down like the man did on that conference call, but you cannot argue in your defense if you're not 100 percent on board with what you're saying.

Say that you have a friend who keeps setting you up with dates. They want to play cupid. You are not on board with this plan. First, metathink through this. (You've gotten this far in the book, so you're obviously great at it now!) Search your feelings—yep, like in Star Wars—and determine exactly where you stand. Like this:

- *What is my friend's point of view here?*
- *Is there a reason they think I want them to do this for me?*
- *Am I being clear? In turn, am I being heard?*
- *Is this a problem, or something I can let go?*
- *This is a problem. How much time do I want to devote to this problem?*

Once you know where you stand and how you feel, you've got a case to build. Here's how:

COLLECT THE EVIDENCE. Know the cold hard facts by heart. You don't want your friend to hook you up with dates, but they texted you that they found your perfect match, even though last week you mentioned that you aren't interested in dating.

SEEK OUTSIDE COUNSEL. Your therapist, a parent, a dear friend, your spouse, an internet pal who doesn't know anyone involved—find someone who will listen generously and build you up after you vent for a few minutes. They can reassure you that no, you aren't irrational because you don't want your friend to hook you up. Your outside counsel can also show you another perspective: Maybe they'll point out that you've wanted to date friends-of-friends in the past, so there's some confusion about what you want right *now*. This is an opportunity to receive a gut check from someone you trust.

FIND A CHARACTER WITNESS. If it makes sense in your situation, privately reach out to a close friend who can advocate for you in the moment—a friend who can gently (or not gently) cut into an uncomfort-able conversation to say, "Hey, Anna isn't interested in our suggestions of who she should date, so that's that." Or "Anna told us that she isn't inter-ested in being set up with anyone, so never mind that idea. Board games, anybody?"

STAGE A MOCK TRIAL. Talk through the conversation in your head and envision a scenario where this goes smoothly. Imagine another scenario where you have to repeat yourself. Plan what you'll say, but remember that you don't need to deliver a sophisticated monologue here. You don't *actually* have to work as hard at this as a professional litigator would. Those TV lawyers have entire writers' rooms devoted to making them sound badass. You just have yourself—and that's enough.

After you've completed these steps, all you should have to do is tell your friend what you need in one or two sentences. Those sentences are now your thesis. If your friend asks you more than once (and we hope they don't), simply repeat or restate your thesis. Avoid casual

Dear Friendshipping,

I'm an event photographer, and my friend wants me to shoot her upcoming wedding. I know in my heart this is a bad idea for our friendship, so I politely told her that I don't photograph weddings for friends (which is true for the most part). However, she does not seem to be taking my answer seriously. How can I be more clear that I am not the right person for this?

It sounds like your friend is going to keep asking you until she gets the answer she wants. What a bummer position to put you in! It's time for an unambiguous statement:

- *I'm not going to be the photographer at your wedding, but I'd love to be a guest!*

- *I feel like you're holding out hope that I'll change my mind, but I want to be clear: This is not something that I am going to do.*

- *I didn't feel heard the last time we talked, so I wanted to make sure you knew that I am not going to shoot your wedding.*

- *I'm not going to be your photographer. I can tell this isn't the answer you wanted, but I'm firm on this.*

At this point, you've made your needs known. Any argument she puts up from here on is an attempt to wear you down, which is rude as hell. Maybe you personally can forgive this because she's planning a wedding and probably under a lot of stress, but still—good friends respect your boundaries.

phrases like "well, maybe" or "eh" or "naaaah, I dunno." This is the time to plainly state what you need, in a tone of voice that feels right for you. Use statements that start with the word "I." *I would prefer; I need / I don't need; I am interested / not interested; I am not willing / I am willing;* and so on. Here are a few ways to make your preferences crystal clear:

- *Hi, Friend, I would prefer if you didn't hook me up with anyone right now. If I change my mind on that in the future, I'll let you know.*
- *I was interested in dating friends-of-friends before, but I changed my mind. Everyone, update your personal files on me.*
- *I'm not into the idea of going out with people my friends set me up with.*
- *I'm glad to hear it's no big deal to you, but I still don't want you to hook me up with anyone. Thank you for being cool about this.*
- *Please stop trying to set me up on dates. I'm just not into it.*

And you don't have to be perfect at this. If your friend does not drop the convo and keeps pressuring you to give the answer they like more, you can ignore the topic at hand and instead acknowledge the weird and unfair situation that they're putting you in. This will feel awkward, of course, but try to accept the awkwardness. You have endured hundreds of awkward moments in your life, and still here you are. Besides, you have not created the awkwardness—your friend has! You can reply:

- *I wish we could drop this subject.*
- *Well, I sure feel weird now.*
- *I heard you the first and second time you brought this up.*

• *Honestly, I'm not sure why you're this interested in my dating life.*

Plus, something to think about: How often do you have to stick up for yourself around your friends? You may be subconsciously seeking out people who pressure you. If so, you may need to do a spring cleaning of the people in your life. Friends should not prioritize their wants over your needs.

PARTING WAYS WITH OLD FRIENDS

We've heard from a lot of listeners who have experienced a significant life change, looked around at their group of friends, and decided now is the time to leave 'em in a cloud of dust. This is a big moment! It's a major decision! We don't tend to advocate in favor of CTRL + ALT + DELETING most things, especially not lots of people at once—unless they are toxic, mistreating you, enabling poor behaviors, or making you feel unsafe. In that case, you do what you gotta do (see page 195). For the less dire cases, though, we're going to ask you to pause juuust a second. Let's first explore options *other* than leaving people permanently behind. When it comes to cutting people from your life, we want you to go into it with your eyes wide open so you'll have zero regrets regarding such an important decision.

First, why slash and burn? What is it about the friend group that is making you want to leave all of them behind? Let's get this possibility out of the way first: It could be that you are trying to run away from your own behavior. People do this. But it's not OK to hurt people and then ignore the aftermath and leave. (Plus, whatever new friend group you join will eventually have conflict, too.) But if this doesn't resonate with you, perhaps you simply need to place some parameters on the friendships. You could:

FIND DIFFERENT THINGS YOU CAN DO TOGETHER. Maybe they party and you don't particularly enjoy partying. Or maybe it's the opposite—you've gotten into dance floors and dive bars and that's not their scene. Make them aware of your new preferences and present them with the idea of something different. Maybe some of them will be interested, and you can start an offshoot group.

TAKE AN EXTENDED BREAK FROM THIS GROUP OF PEOPLE. A trial separation period could be all you need. See what your life feels like without them; fill your social calendar with different people. We suggest giving your friends a heads-up so they aren't startled or worried that you are being unresponsive. A text message could accomplish this: "Hey, friends, I'm going to [take a social break / get some rest / do some mental housekeeping] so I'll be absent for the next few weeks." Maybe don't add "nothing is wrong, everything is fine" because you don't quite know if that's true yet. Pepper in a few thumbs-up emojis instead.

CHANGE HOW YOU INTERACT WITH THEM. Is it the behavior of the group that needs adjusting? This is a common problem in old friend groups—the kind that formed when you were in diapers or in junior

Dear Friendshipping,

A beloved teacher from my high school passed away suddenly. Her death made me think very hard about the person I want to be going forward, and I decided to make a lot of changes. I got a new hairdo, a new job, and I left my partner of six years. I write more, I go outdoors more, I go "out" more. I eat that extra slice of cake, and I drink that extra glass of wine. I'm so much happier. But my friends still know me as the Old Me. How do I let go of them and find myself a squad that better fits the New Me?

Keep doing your thing! You are going to new places and meeting all kinds of new people. Be your sparkling new self. But do you need to "let go" of anyone? You can have many friends, and friendships can have pauses or dry spells. It's possible to explore new relationships without salting the lands behind you. It's OK to want distance from people who make you feel trapped in an old identity, but you also haven't mentioned anything specifically bad or alarming about your old friend group. For now we encourage you to get additional friends, rather than a replacement set.

high school. The immature or outdated behavior (roasting one another, making rude jokes, whacking one another in the testicles) has been grandfathered into your interactions, and now you would like it to stop. That's certainly reasonable. You can adjust the settings on your friendship operating system.

HANG OUT ONE-ON-ONE, RATHER THAN IN A BIG GROUP. Even if the old friend group isn't working out for you, maybe you have a special bond with one of its members. Try replanting that friendship in a new context. On the TV show *Big Dreams Small Spaces,* when gardener Monty Don works on a backyard, he doesn't dig out every plant—he first examines what is there to see if they can be improved or successfully replanted elsewhere in the garden. Same idea here: You can upcycle your friends.

LOOK AT THE HISTORY OF YOUR FRIENDSHIP. Your shared history with a group of friends cannot be replaced. There's something unique and precious about friendships that span decades and identities. If you think it's worth holding on to, give the group an opportunity to grow and change along with you.

Jumping ship should be the last option, one that you use guiltlessly but do not take lightly. Leaving friends behind may be the best and truest path for you, but our point is simply this: Deleting people shouldn't be the go-to move. You can instead edit their place in your life.

WHEN FRIENDS GHOST YOU

Your friend hasn't initiated plans in months; your last five text messages have gone unanswered; another phone call went to voicemail. What gives? Well, no one enjoys hearing this, but it is completely possible—as great as you are—that a friend might simply drift away from you. It really is not as rare or shocking as it seems. In fact, befriending someone for life is what's rare!

Life piles on so many stresses that socializing often gets shoved to the very bottom of the to-do list. Perhaps your friend is in "survival mode"—they are tackling pressing responsibilities and don't have an ounce of energy to spare. If your friend, say, has a loved one in the hospital or is frantically hunting for a new job, answering even one text might demand too much of their frayed attention. Or maybe it's less dire, and your friend simply put their head down to finish their dissertation without distraction. Maybe they are dating someone new and are deep in that honeymoon spend-all-their-time-together phase. Or they could be off the grid because they dunked their phone in the toilet. You can privately speculate about what's going on with your friend, but here's

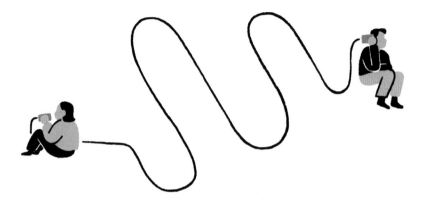

the thing: The reason for their absence—whatever it is—doesn't matter right now. You're still going to proceed in the same fashion: patiently, cautiously, and mindfully.

STEP 1: Reach out with a very clear invitation and very clear plans. Suggest an activity that doesn't require much time, commitment, commuting, or planning. If you previously suggested going to Six Flags, camping for a weekend, or putting together a cross-country road trip, the activity itself is likely a problem. Invite them to catch up over a quick coffee / sandwich / beer instead. Something low-key. If they turn down this invitation, reply to the tune of, "Hey, no big deal, sounds like things are busy for you. How about you get in touch with me when you're available?" Or "No problem. Just let me know when you've got time!"

STEP 2: If you don't hear from them in, like, a week (or a month, or some length of time that feels comfortable to you based on how often you interact with them otherwise), attempt one final shot at getting on their social calendar. Just one! If they decline, you can explain: "Bummer, I would've really liked to see you since it has been so long! No worries. I'll leave the ball in your court. Just reach out when you want to hang."

No guilt trips here, but you can make it clear that their presence and absence mean something to you.

STEP 3: That's it! Now is the time to back away. Focus your energy on more immediate company, and don't issue more invitations or leave more comments than usual on their social media feeds. Give this person the space that they are obviously asking for.

At that point, you have taken all the correct steps, and you've given this friend the chance to opt in to your company or explain their

Dear Friendshipping,

I think my friend is just too busy for me. There could be a variety of reasons for this: We're both in our late twenties, we both have other people we need to take care of / want to spend time with. He's got a lot going on between his day job and his hefty creative side job, but we have always made time for each other. At this point we haven't seen each other in probably a month, and it's been almost that long since we have had a meaningful conversation. Should I still ask him to hang out? Am I being unreasonable?

Work, side work, adulthood responsibilities—you've made an excellent list of reasons why you and your friend haven't seen each other. With all these complications, it's understandable that your friend has been absent. You're not unreasonable for feeling alone and missing your friend, but it also doesn't sound like this is his fault, or that he's creating this distance on purpose. What specific change would you like to see? "I wish you would make time for me" is a difficult ask, but "Let's catch up over a cold one next Tuesday evening if your schedule allows" sounds inviting and considerate, doesn't it? Attempt to make a concrete plan with your friend, and try to be understanding if he can't make it work.

absence. They know how to reach you. If this works out and you do hang out with your friend again, great. Use the lessons you learned about your friend—like they're on a budget so they're never going to say yes to hangouts that cost money, or they have a limited social battery—to make better-suited plans in the future. But if this doesn't work out, and you don't end up seeing your friend (they are unresponsive, they decline the invitation), then you know it's the right time to let go.

When this happens, especially when you're not given a reason, you're left with confusion, unanswered questions, and feelings of hurt. But there are dozens of serious and well-founded reasons why your friend walked out that are not about you at all:

- Your friendship (rightly or wrongly!) represents a difficult or embarrassing time in this person's life that they'd like to leave behind. This is common with people who leave behind their high school, college, or work friends.
- Someone else tangential to you (like a mutual friend) might have acted badly or abusively toward this person, so they need distance. Your friend doesn't want to make waves, and they just need to take care of themselves first and foremost.
- They are having a crisis of identity. They may need to remove themselves from outside influences to figure out who they are.

But they also might have felt like the friendship just wasn't right for them, and they didn't want to explain that to you. There are no scripts for this kind of thing. There's no precedent. People are so much more likely to seize upon the most uncomplicated, least awkward option. In this case, that means drifting away rather than returning your calls to explain, "I can't make this friendship a priority." In a small, strange way, perhaps ghosting is a gift for you, too: You don't have to endure an awkward conversation.

Still, we know this hurts. Try to take comfort in the fact that although unenjoyable, it *is* common—you *will* be ghosted at some point in your life (if it hasn't happened already), and you ought to let people ghost you. Let people leave without confrontation and major conflict. Allow people to make their graceful exits, even when it feels unfair or makes you sad. You can't convince anyone to be your companion, nor should you, and you don't need this one person as your friend to make you worthy of plenty of other friendships.

POISON CONTROL: HOW TO END A TOXIC FRIENDSHIP

What does it mean to be a toxic friend? Toxicity is not messing up once or twice. It's more than a handful of hurtful mistakes. In fact, you can make pretty significant fuck-ups and still not be a toxic friend. Every single one of us has acted badly. We've all been the shitty friend. We're imperfect creatures who are subject to sour moods, quick judgments, and selfish decisions. It would be unreasonable to expect yourself or anyone else to always be a perfect friend. But toxic behavior is a pattern of mistreatment over time. Red flags for this—never mind the name— are not easy to see. In fact, they are often expertly hidden. A friend can seem downright warm and nice while repeatedly mistreating you (and would not categorize their actions as mistreatment).

If a friend is perpetrating one or more of these behaviors time and time again, that's a flashing warning signal. Toxic friends consistently:

- Take advantage of people, especially those who are quiet, flexible, or lenient

- Make others feel stressed, anxious, and powerless
- Refuse to take no for an answer
- Compete aggressively with their friends
- Act rudely, insensitively, or negatively
- Prioritize their own wants over other peoples' needs
- Ignore clear social cues
- Blame other people for their bad mood and mistakes
- Sulk when something doesn't go exactly their way
- Lecture, shame, or belittle friends for their choices or beliefs
- Make other people feel guilty for having fun without them
- Insist that they deserve apologies, but rarely, if ever, make apologies themselves
- Punish people with the cold shoulder
- Pick apart friends' appearances, outfits, and body types
- Interrupt people to talk about themselves
- Initiate exaggerated, excessive fights

- Show little or no interest in what doesn't involve them
- Reach out with the most enthusiasm when they need a favor or want something
- Attempt to control the details, conversation, and nuances of social situations
- Express jealousy or resentment when people hang out without them
- Act like the victim in situations where they are the one causing harm
- Unload their problems without listening to others in return

We could never possibly share every shade of toxicity because toxic people are not easy to notice. Life would be easier if monsters always looked like monsters, but they don't. Sometimes, they look like our friends. Your friend probably has redeeming qualities alongside the toxicity—they might be [fun to go to the bar with every Friday / your helpful chemistry tutor / your closest friend in the city / an old friend of your family / your backpacking buddy when you travel abroad / the person you spend holidays with]. Toxic friends walk among us every day, and while they are not rare, they are sometimes hard to spot.

If you've ever observed a toxic friendship as a bystander, you've probably wanted to yell, "Why are you still friends?! Ditch that mofo!" If only it was that easy. Pulling away from a toxic person feels like moving a mountain with your hands—impossible. That's what makes this situation so poisonous. You feel trapped. But you *can* end the friendship or build protective boundaries around yourself. Even if you think you are a doormat. Even if you're an extreme people-pleaser. Maybe you will decide it's not worth the effort to extract or protect yourself, but know that you can always make decisions and choices in your friendships, no matter how powerless you feel. Here are some of your possibilities:

PRIVILEGE, TOXICITY, AND EDUCATING YOUR FRIENDS (OR NOT)

Here's a damn good reason to cut someone from your life: They are racist, sexist, or otherwise mistreating a person or a group of people. If your privilege and relationship with that person allow you to safely do so, consider educating them on why their actions are harmful and unacceptable before you leave them behind. After all, society benefits when people are made aware that there are, in fact, consequences (losing you as a friend, losing your respect, losing your trust) to their shitty behavior. However, if you're the injured party, you do not have to take responsibility for someone else's education. You have only so much time on this planet, and you do not have to spend your limited energy telling Karen yet again that it's disrespectful when she touches your hair, or explaining to Bliff why his "ironic" sexist cracks aren't actually funny, or repeatedly reminding Chud why pronouns matter. If you are *not* the injured party—you're a dude who doesn't want to be friends with a misogynist, or a white person who doesn't want to be friends with a racist—please consider taking on the work of educating this person. Your words as a member of a privileged class carry weight. You have a voice and a responsibility to use it.

YOU CAN REESTABLISH TERMS AND BOUNDARIES. Boundaries are not unkind, nor are they impolite. Sharing your boundaries is a gracious act because it means that you might see a way forward with this friendship. When you have decided on yours, share them. If you already shared them and they went ignored (ugh), that does not mean your boundaries are "wrong" or that you should have kept quiet. If you want to, restate them more firmly than you ever have before: You can tell this friend they are mistreating you, how they are mistreating you, and that there are consequences when they mistreat you. Lay out an "if/then" scenario, like this: "Friend, you know that I do not drink alcohol, and I need you to stop pressuring me to drink and stay out late with you. This is a *need*. If this doesn't stop, I can't join you at [bars / restaurants / parties]." Or "After what you said on Saturday, I have decided that we cannot hang out just the two of us anymore. We can only hang out in groups." Or "I need you to stop making me feel bad for [hanging out with other people / my spiritual life / prioritizing my job over going to a concert with you / my decision to not have children]. This is nonnegotiable. Until you can promise me this, our friendship is going to suffer." Think of this as building a tall, protective, and necessary fence around yourself. Without a fence, this friend can get close and hurt you. But from now on, you are not going to allow this friend to get inside your front yard unless it's safe to do so, at which time you will unlock the gate yourself.

YOU CAN SEND A FINAL MESSAGE. Provide a concise written explanation before cutting them out: "I no longer want us to be friends; I am ending this friendship." Or "I have decided to end our friendship. It is not healthy for either of us. Please don't contact me anymore." Or "I need

a long, long break from our friendship. I will reach out when I'm ready."
They're not given the opportunity to talk you out of your decision, make
you feel guilty, or ask for explanations. You don't owe explanations. You
have already given them so much of your time, and time is not something you can ever get back.

YOU CAN UNDERGO A FORMAL BREAKUP. This is a one-on-one, sit-
down kind of conversation where you try to educate the other person
on their behavior and how it has hurt you time and time again, and tell
them you can't continue the friendship because of it. Of course this will
be awkward and painful, but it's because they have forced you into this
situation. It isn't your job to smooth over awkwardness. Understand that
your toxic friend will have the opportunity to refute your claims, try to
make you feel guilty, or tell you you're being too sensitive. They might
weep or become furious; they might apologize or become defensive; they
might snap into reality and realize they need to make changes. And they
might return to their old patterns in a month. The outcome will be hard
to predict. Just know before stepping into this conversation that you do
not need to provide endless polished explanations and justifications.
The fact that you are being mistreated is reason enough for you to speak
up and leave the friendship.

When a reasonable person is confronted with the consequences
of their bad behavior, they might be confused or hurt, but also apologetic
and committed to change. Unfortunately, this friend has proven themselves to be unreasonable—that's the whole reason you're breaking up
with them. So before you begin what will be a very difficult conversation, decide exactly what you want to get out of it. Are you looking for
closure? What are the chances that you'll get it? If you give them an
opportunity to apologize or change and they don't take it, will you feel
even worse? Do you want them to feel hurt, as you do? That's an understandable thing to want, but will it bring you peace in the long run?

How Do I Know If
I'M THE TOXIC FRIEND?

If you earnestly ask yourself this, tremendous props to you. Toxic people rarely entertain the idea of being toxic and spend very little time on self-reflection. Recognizing unhealthy patterns is a step toward overturning them. We know these questions may be difficult to confront, but they might help stir your thoughts. (Notice if any of them are *particularly* difficult to confront—if so, that's a subject worth exploring further.)

- Would you describe any of your friendships as "strained"? What about "complicated"? Why?

- Which friendships need lots of work and upkeep? Why?

- How often do you text or email friends while feeling angry? Look back through your threads and in your "sent" folder. How many emotionally charged messages have you sent in the last year?

- How often do you fight with friends? Do you fight with one friend in particular? Or do you avoid conflict and keep anger to yourself?

- Would you describe yourself as dependable? Do you honor your commitments? How often are you late? How often do you cancel plans, especially on one person in particular?

- When friends are hanging out without you, what do you feel? Sad? Offended? Excluded? Slighted?

- How often do you use the word "should"? Do you give advice? When, and to whom?

- Do you trust your friends to make their own choices?

- Do you feel frustrated when a social event doesn't meet your expectations? In these scenarios, how do you feel? What do you say?

YOU CAN GHOST. Need to leave this friendship ASAP? We give you permission to get the hell out. You can ignore their invitations, disregard their texts, block them on social media, block their number, and remain unresponsive. We know this sounds rude, but it's not rude to take care of yourself. And why do you have to be perfectly polite, while they mistreat and bully you?

Dear Friendshipping,

I have totally lost joy in my friend's company and find myself dreading the time we spend together. We are old friends from childhood, and I finally realized our dynamic is toxic. When we're together, all she does is complain, and I'm expected to take care of her. I don't see how I can just pull away. Even our parents know one another. What do you do if a friendship has become extra stressful?

It's so understandable that you feel pressure to maintain this relationship, despite the fact that this person is awful to hang out with. But you absolutely do not need to remain friends. If your parents know each other, it may even be that you've been forced into the same company in the past. But you're an adult now, and your time is absolutely and unequivocally yours. So, it's time to say no to things. Don't make plans with her. Maintain a healthy distance. When she asks to hang out, you do not need to make excuses—you can simply decline. If pressed, there are many creative ways to tell the truth without directly telling her that you don't like her (which is rarely helpful feedback): "You know, I just haven't felt like hanging out," "I've been taking more time to myself lately," "My schedule is packed."

And, if possible, bring in some support. Is it realistic to tell your parents that you no longer want to be near this person? We hope they will respect your decision. If not, that's a bummer! But you don't need their blessing.

Now, the aftermath. Breaking up with a friend—no matter how you go about it—is not so different from a romantic breakup. You'll probably experience a range of emotions. You are allowed to feel sadness and a sense of loss, because you *have* suffered a loss. Maybe you will feel relieved and free, or maybe you'll get terrible pangs of guilt and you'll worry that you were somehow unkind or unfair. All these feelings are normal, and they are not an indication that you made a mistake. You are grieving—give yourself time and space to heal. Treat yourself to whatever makes you feel good: a nice meal, a strong beer, a long nap, a movie, a walk. Be incredibly kind to yourself in the weeks that follow, because you deserve that. Time will help you make sense of these emotions. Other ideas that could help move you toward a happier place:

- Going to therapy
- Writing down your thoughts, especially as they change and evolve
- Laughing really hard at comedy podcasts, stand-up specials, or YouTube videos
- Blasting sad, angry, or happy breakup songs (even if they're about romantic breakups, many lyrics will still apply)
- Talking to a loving friend, sibling, or parent
- Throwing yourself into new hobbies
- Updating or reorganizing something that brings you joy (your bookcase, living room furniture, makeup collection, board game shelf)
- Enjoying all the free time you have now that you aren't giving it to a toxic person

If you and your ex-friend have mutual buds, you may want to give them a heads-up about your newfound status (but you're not required to explain your decision to anyone unless you want to). If you decide it's right for you, here are scripts for you to edit:

- *So, Celeste and I are taking a break from our friendship. Maybe permanently. I just wanted you to know. You don't have to change how you treat me or how you treat Celeste.*
- *I ended my friendship with Tom because they treated me badly and [here's how].*
- *Can you let me know if Isabelle will be at your party? I am asking because she and I are not friends anymore. Nothing we need to discuss—I'm moving on and doing just fine—but I may skip the party if Isabelle is there, just for everyone's sake. You and I can hang out another time!*
- *Good evening, friends. C.J. and I are divorced from friend-marriage due to irreconcilable differences. Basically, we aren't hanging out anymore. I will not be taking questions at this time. Please direct all further inquiries to my publicist. Thanks! That's all.*

From there, your friends might talk among themselves, have questions, show concern, or express confusion and surprise. It's natural for them to have opinions or questions. But you don't need anyone's approval to end a toxic friendship, and you're not required to give them any more information than you're comfortable with. You don't have to field and dodge questions like you're holding a press conference. We hope you have friends who will treat you with respect, and that they will accept this information and move on. If instead they accuse you of "causing drama" or shame you for taking measures to protect yourself, they are in the wrong. You're shutting down a harmful and upsetting situation. You're closing the door and locking it safely behind you. Is there someone you know you can trust in the group, a friend you are very close to? If so, lean on that person to help you navigate the group dynamics from here on out. Quite frankly, there's a chance that one or more of your friends will cheer you on. There's even a possibility that you start a mass migration away from a person who needs to make major changes. This might in fact be the thing that gets that person to change. Don't *expect* this outcome, but you never know.

As you move on, be prepared for conflicting emotions. One day you might consider this person your mortal enemy, and the next, you're looking back fondly on your old jokes and routines. You might sometimes forget that they were ever a monster at all and find yourself missing their company. It's not a sign that you should rekindle the friendship, but it's understandable to feel this way. This person made a significant impact on your life and you miss the good parts. It's OK to miss a monster, but please—don't feed yourself to the monster.

• • •

When Marie Kondo discards an old article of clothing from her wardrobe, she thanks it for its service in her life. Even if she buys a shirt and immediately regrets the purchase, she thanks the garment for teaching her what not to buy in the future. Like the great Ms. Kondo, you now know yourself better, and your closet is cleaner. So much more of the world is open to you when you remove a toxic relationship from your life. The time you spent stressed and worried, the energy you expended trying to build yourself back up when they tore you down—they're yours again. You are now in a new universe of possibility. The difficult and necessary housekeeping is behind you, and you're free to move forward in the best way you can.

"*If you want to support others
you have to stay upright yourself.*"

—PETER HØEG

A Final Note:
ON KINDNESS

Great news: You just finished reading a book about friendship. You are the kind of person who sets aside their limited time and energy to get better at caring about people. You spent at least several hours thinking about the way you communicate and what you can do to more thoughtfully navigate your relationships. (Or you skipped to the end of the book to see what we're about. That's still a good sign.)

So if there's one single lesson we have learned through our personal friendships and making our podcast together that we'd like to pass on above all else, it's this: Being kind—to ourselves, our friends, the people around us—is not always easy. If it were easy, surely we would encounter more of it each day. Being kind is difficult because *life* is difficult. When you choose to be kind, you are fighting your own hurt and your own trauma, and all the bad habits and judgments you've been taught since birth. It means admitting your failures and wrongdoings and choosing to learn from people who are different from you. (Of course, you do not have to be courteous and polite to people who do not deserve it. Sometimes the greatest act of self-kindness is distancing yourself from those people.)

And know this: You won't be kind every day. It's something to strive and reach for, and sometimes you'll fall short. But you *do* have to put in the effort. For as long as you are alive. Because the only way you can guarantee that you will contribute to the sum of goodness on the planet is by being a kind person. Over and over again, we have felt astounded by the kindness of our friends:

When Trin was out of town and having a few intense, sad days, Savannah sent her photos of Trin's cats and wrote a letter from their perspective, including how much they love her, how they have all gotten through so much, and how they have so much to look forward to together.

Jenn ran cross country in college. She was not particularly good at it. This did not stop a crowd of her friends from showing up on race day to cheer in rainy thirty-five-degree weather in homemade T-shirts with bare chests painted.

When Trin was experiencing a particularly nasty bout of online harassment, her friends sent a cake to her door that read SORRY THE INTERNET IS BAD.

In the early days of writing this book, Jenn complained to Kunal over whiskey at 2:00 a.m. that writing was proving difficult and she wished someone would appear once a week to tell her to keep working on it. In response, Kunal took his phone from his pocket, set a reminder for himself, and called Jenn weekly to ask, "Hey, you writing yet?" (You're reading this, so you know how this turned out.)

Sometimes it feels like kindness is limited, like it's gone missing in a dark world. But we know that kindness survives, because we have friends who show us. You can be that example of kindness for someone else. Your friendship is a gift. Now go out and give it to someone who will treasure it.

RESOURCES

Code Switch
A weekly podcast exploring how race intersects every aspect of our lives
NPR.org/sections/codeswitch

Project Implicit
An exercise in knowing your biases, The Implicit Association Test measures associations between concepts and evaluations or stereotypes
Implicit.Harvard.edu/implicit/takeatest.html

Charity Navigator
An independent organization that evaluates charities and nonprofit organizations; a helpful tool in deciding where to donate or volunteer
CharityNavigator.org

The following are resources for those located in the United States:

National Suicide Prevention Lifeline
Call 1-800-273-8255
SuicidePreventionLifeline.org
Includes online chat options

National Domestic Violence Hotline
Call 1-800-799-7233
TheHotline.org
Includes online chat options

Rape, Abuse & Incest National Network (RAINN)
Call 1-800-656-4673 to reach the National Sexual Assault Hotline
RAINN.org
Includes online chat options

National Alliance on Mental Illness

NAMI.org

Advice on finding mental health treatment that fits your cultural background

BetterHelp

BetterHelp.com

Online counseling and therapist matching

Anxiety and Depression Association of America

ADAA.org

Online support groups and discussion, therapist matching

Psychology Today

PsychologyToday.com

Therapists and psychologists in your zip code and insurance information

Without My Consent

WithoutMyConsent.org

Tools and guidance for victims of online harassment and privacy violations

ACKNOWLEDGMENTS

From Jenn

This book and so much else would not be possible without Nadija, who has been an unfailing support since elementary school. I also owe tremendous gratitude to Lynne, who makes every day better, funnier, and brighter, and always has. Terri and everyone in Team Slytherin, you make life so much fun.

Thank you for your mentorship, Jane; for your parables, Nick; and thank you, Melissa, for always giving me a ride home, literally and figuratively. Mr. Hochstetler and Coach Begley, the world needs more people as generous as you both.

Growing up, my parents never seemed to miss a track meet or orchestra concert, and my older brother Chris always encouraged me to be my truest self, no matter how weird that person was. I am forever grateful for their support.

Jon, thank you for your patience, your strength, and for filling our lives with happiness. This is for you.

From Trin

Andy, your godlike and unkillable friendship spits in the face of probability. Conal, let's laugh and grow and make weird art together forever. Thanks to Gus, Karlyn, the Pod Squad, and SteVen, who taught me how to accept friendship and how to be a friend. Thank you to Mr. Anstett, Mr. Bultman, and Mrs. E. Carroll, who taught me school stuff. And thank you to the crack team of therapists, psychiatrists, and pharmacists who have successfully kept me alive this long.

From both of us

We are forever indebted to Ian for producing and editing our podcast; Monika, Rachael, Sun, Ashley, Becky, Barbara, Beth, Erica, Cindy, Emily, and Jean for their tireless efforts; Karlyn for her wisdom; and Molly, Pat, Lauren, Alex, and LoadingReadyRun for all their help. If you made it here from our podcast, thank you for reading. You're welcome for writing.